BEAR ISLAND

OCEAN

Politica[l]

BARENTS SEA

Bardufoss · Petsamo
KOLA
PENINSULA
vik

Lulea ·

GULF OF BOTHNIA

FINLAND

· LENINGRAD

ESTONIA

U. S. S. R.

· MOSCOW

LATVIA
Memel · LITHUANIA

WHITE
RUSSIA

EAST
PRUSSIA

OLAND

· WARSAW

Stalingrad ·

CASPIAN
SEA

eiwitz
Teschen CARPATHIAN MNTS
AKIA
OVAKIA RUTHENIA

UKRAINE

NGARY

RUMANIA

BELGRADE
GOSLAVIA
BULGARIA

BLACK SEA

ALBANIA
BALKANS

GREECE

TURKEY

SYRIA

NEAN SEA

LEBANON

PALESTINE JORDAN

# Anthony Farrar-Hockley

# OPENING ROUNDS

## LESSONS OF
## MILITARY HISTORY
## 1918–1988

ANDRE DEUTSCH

First published 1988 by
André Deutsch Limited
105–106 Great Russell Street
London WC1B 3LJ

British Library Cataloguing in Publication Data
Farrar-Hockley, *Sir* Anthony
  Opening Rounds.
  Lessons of Military History 1918–1988
  1. Military art and science
  I. Title
  355'.02'01        U102

ISBN 0–233–98009–1

Typeset by David John Services Ltd, Slough
Printed in Great Britain by St Edmundsbury Press Ltd
Bury St Edmunds, Suffolk

# CONTENTS

# ACKNOWLEDGEMENTS

I acknowledge with thanks the assistance of the United Kingdom Public Record Office, Kew, the Foreign and Commonwealth Office Library and the London Library; in Washington DC, the National Archives, the Library of Congress and the Historical Office of the Department of State. Acknowledgement is also due to the many organizations whose publications I have drawn upon in preparation of this work; full details of sources used are given in the Select Bibliography at the end of the book.

Among numerous individuals who kindly gave me advice, I owe special thanks to Professor Olav Riste´and Professor Emeritus Magne Skodvin of the University of Oslo, Professor Hisao Iwashima, former Director of the Department of Military History in Tokyo, Christopher Donnelly and the Soviet Studies Centre, Sandhurst, and John Andrews and the Ministry of Defence Library.

'If men could learn from history, what lessons it might teach us! But passion and party blind our eyes, and the light which experience gives is a lantern on the stern, which shines only on the waves behind us.'

Samuel Taylor Coleridge
(From T. Alsop's *Recollections*)

# INTRODUCTION

After a period of peace, the citizens of democracies find it difficult
to believe that they may become engaged in war. Distant campaigns
involving their own servicemen may intrude upon their conscious-
ness via the television screen but are not much more of a reality
than the movie which follows the news. Both will fade when the set
is switched off. War which engulfs the homeland and its people is
quite another matter. The governments of Europe allowed themselves to drift into war in 1914; and at the end of it, surveying the
monstrous loss of life and suffering, the whole society of the world,
it seemed, vowed that they should not be endured again. Twenty
years later, a second world war began. The progressively plain aims
and methods of the aggressors had been at first disregarded and
then tolerated as other peoples' business in these intervening years
by Britain and its associated dominions, France, the United States,
the Low Countries, Denmark and Norway, until it was too late.
Then they were obliged to engage in the opening rounds of a war
for which they were unprepared morally, professionally and
materially. It is not surprising that they were trounced and, in some
cases, brought under brutal occupation by their foes. Prolonged
suffering and loss were the consequences. Victory and peace for the
surviving victims of aggression were secured only after prodigious
effort when, once more, war was foresworn as a means of solving
international problems in a general assembly of sovereign states.

Within two or three years of this gathering and this declaration, a
third world war was a distinct possibility. Once-free peoples such as
the Czechs or Poles had been subjugated by the Soviet Union under
the umbrella of the Red Army. There is abundant evidence that this
process was to be extended by politico-military coercion into
northern and western Europe. The prize there was the wealth of
material resources – to be carried off under the one-sided trading

xi

terms familiar to Soviet satellite nations – and the consolidation of Soviet political power; aims broadly similar to those of Germany and Japan between the wars. As openly as – perhaps more so than – the Nazi arrogation of universal leadership, the hierarchy of the Soviet Union had declared itself to be the principal in the extension of Communism throughout the world. There is little reason to suppose that Russian aims have changed if they can be secured at an acceptable price involving, if necessary, armed struggle.

For more than thirty years that price has been too high. The Atlantic Alliance, incorporating the United States and Canada with the majority of European democracies, has ensured that no country can be picked off singly by the threat or act of war. The development of atomic weapons has added a terrifying complement to the range of arms held as a deterrent to aggression. Thirty years on, the peoples of these democracies once more find it difficult to believe in the possibility of war. As pressures on budgets grow and the ethos of liberalism extends, this incredulity encourages governments in the Alliance to take risks with defence, cutting outlays while pretending to maintain comprehensive capabilities – on the road to disposing, as Bismarck once jibed, 'a lath of wood painted to look like iron'.

It may now be of mutual interest to East and West to reduce these capabilities. The persistent economic difficulties of the Soviet Union have impelled it to negotiate for disarmament on a more realistic basis. But the members of the Atlantic Alliance should heed the lessons implicit in their memorials to those lost in two world wars, and in the Korean War. As the following pages manifest, disarmament which changes the balance of forces adversely for those dedicated to defence does not reduce the risk of war but enhances it. If this is a statement of the obvious, it was not obvious in Washington, Paris or London between the two world wars.

Lest we forget.

# LIST OF MAPS

1. Political Boundaries in Europe 1919–39
2. The Campaign in Poland 1939
3. Operations in Norway 1940
4. Political Boundaries in East Asia 1940
5. Malaya 1941
6. The Philippines 1941
7. Political Boundaries in Europe post-1945

*Cartography by Sue Lawes*

# Political Boundaries in Europe 1919~39

BEAR ISLAND

OCEAN

BARENTS SEA

Bardufoss
vik
Petsamo
KOLA PENINSULA

FINLAND

Lulea

GULF OF BOTHNIA

LENINGRAD

ESTONIA

U. S. S. R.

LATVIA
MOSCOW

Memel LITHUANIA

EAST PRUSSIA

WHITE RUSSIA

OLAND

WARSAW

Stalingrad

CASPIAN SEA

eiwitz
Teschen CARPATHIAN MNTS
AKIA
OVAKIA RUTHENIA

UKRAINE

NGARY

RUMANIA

BELGRADE

GOSLAVIA

ALBANIA

BALKANS

BULGARIA

BLACK SEA

GREECE

TURKEY

NEAN
SEA

SYRIA

LEBANON

PALESTINE JORDAN

MAP 2

SWEDEN

NORWA

NORTH

SEA

DENMARK

GREAT BRITAIN

POME

HOLLAND

GERMANY

BELGIUM

RHINELAND
(RE-MILITARISED)

SUDETENLAND

BOH

E

LUXEMBOURG

BAVARIA

FRANCE

Berchtesga

AUSTRI

SWITZERLAND

ITALY

0          100MILES
0          160KMS

# The Campaign in Poland 1939

ESTONIA

BALTIC SEA

LATVIA

Memel

LITHUANIA

WHITE

RUSSIA

Danzig

EAST PRUSSIA

U. S. S. R.

Tuchel
Plevno
Swetch

Vistula

Warsaw

POLAND

SILESIA

Vistula

San

Bug

UKRAINE

MORAVIA

SLOVAKIA

SLOVAKIA

CARPATHIAN MOUNTAINS

HUNGARY

RUMANIA

YUGOSLAVIA

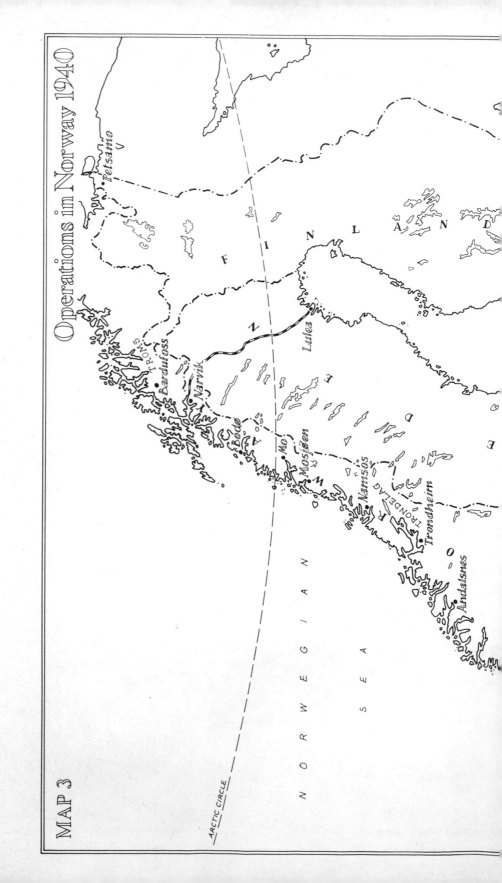

MAP 3

Operations in Norway 1940

ARCTIC CIRCLE

N O R W E G I A N   S E A

Petsamo

F I N L A N D

TROMS

Bardufoss

Narvik

Bodø

Mo

Mosjøen

Namsos

Lulea

TRONDELAG

Trondheim

Andalsnes

100 MILES

160 KMS

0

0

SEA

BALTIC

N

OSLO

FORNEBU AIRFIELD

Oslo Fjord

Stavanger

SOLA AIRFIELD

Lillesand

Kristiansand

Skagerrak

Jøsing Fjord

Kattegat

Aalborg

JUTLAND

DENMARK

COPENHAGEN

Kiel

Hamburg

Bay of Wilhelmshaven

NORTH  SEA

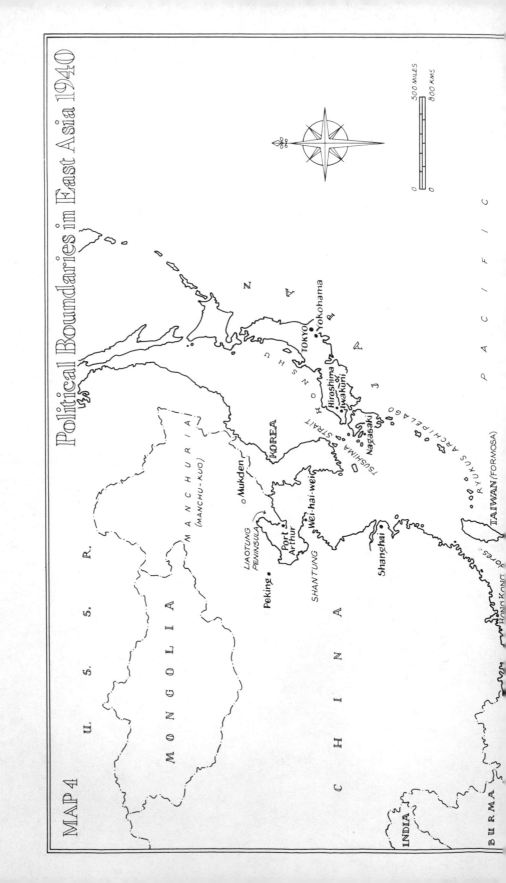

MAP 4

Political Boundaries in East Asia 1940

U. S. S. R.

MONGOLIA

MANCHURIA
(MANCHU-KUO)

N

o Mukden

LIAOTUNG
PENINSULA

Peking •

Port
Arthur •

KOREA

Wei-hai-wei •

SHANTUNG

C H I N A

Shanghai •

HONSHU

TOKYO •
• Yokohama

Hiroshima
o•
Iwakuni

Nagasaki •

TSUSHIMA STRAIT

J A P A N

RYUKYUS ARCHIPELAGO

TAIWAN (FORMOSA)

P A C I F I C

BURMA

INDIA

HONG KONG

500 MILES

800 KMS

0

0

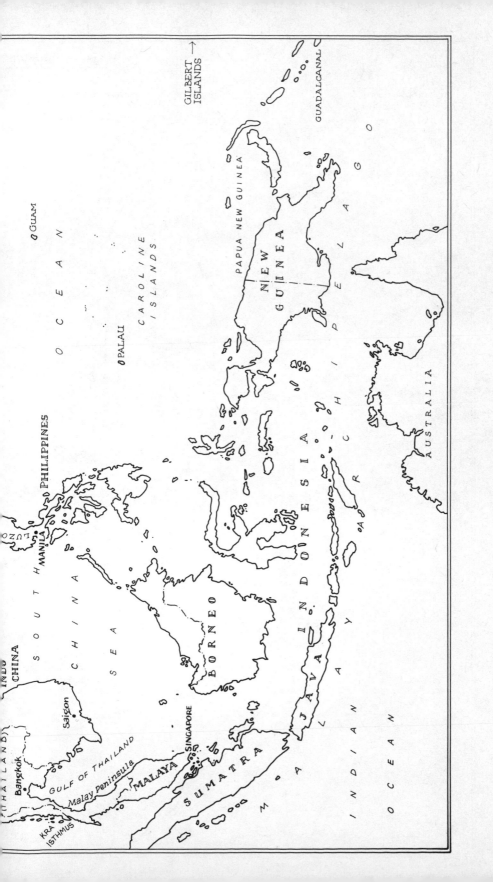

MAP 5

Malaya 1941

THAILAND

+ *River Crossing*

Singora

Patani

PERLIS
Jitra

Alor Star

Kota Bharu

KEDAH

PROVINCE
WELLESLEY

PENANG

TRENGANNU

PERAK

MALAYA

Perak

PAHANG

Kuantan

STRAITS

SELANGOR

NEGRI
SEMBILAN

SETTLEMENTS

MALACCA

JOHORE

DUTCH EAST

MALAYA

SINGAPORE

INDIES POSSESSION

0          50 MILES

0          80 KMS

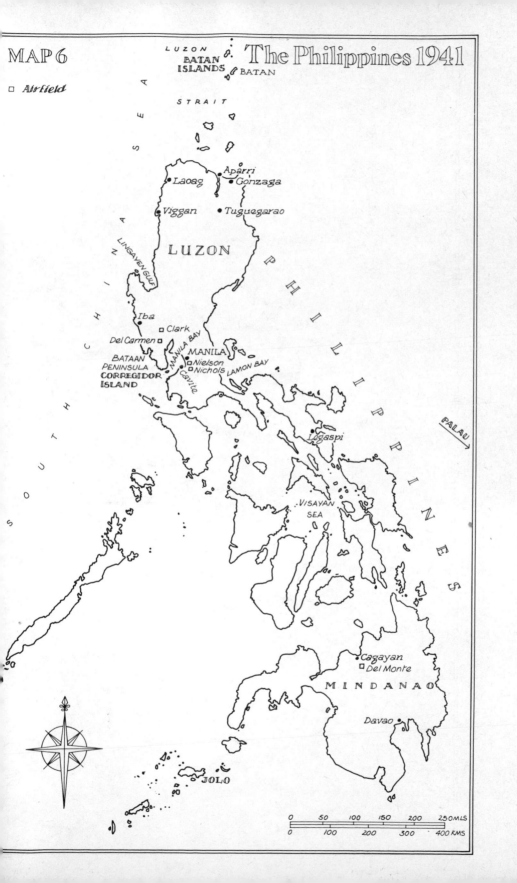

MAP 6       The Philippines 1941

□ *Airfield*

LUZON
BATAN
ISLANDS
BATAN

S T R A I T

Aparri
Laoag   Gonzaga

Viggan   Tuguegarao

L U Z O N

LINGAYEN GULF

Iba
Clark
Del Carmen

MANILA
Nielson
Nichols
Cavite

MANILA BAY
LAMON BAY

BATAAN
PENINSULA
CORREGIDOR
ISLAND

S O U T H   C H I N A   S E A

Legaspi

PALAU

VISAYAN
SEA

P H I L I P P I N E S

M I N D A N A O

Cagayan
Del Monte

Davao

JOLO

0   50   100   150   200   250 MLS
0   100   200   300   400 KMS

Political Boundaries in
Europe post~1945

BEAR ISLAND

OCEAN

BARENTS SEA

Pachenga (Petsamo)

Murmansk
KOLA
PENINSULA

FINLAND

NATO member countries

Warsaw Pact countries

Neutral countries

U. S. S. R.

BYELORUSSIA
(WHITE RUSSIA)

•Chernobyl

LAND

CARPATHIAN MTS

AKIA

NGARY

RUMANIA

CASPIAN SEA

GOSLAVIA

BULGARIA

BLACK SEA

ALBANIA

BALKANS

GREECE

TURKEY

SYRIA

EAN SEA

LEBANON

JORDAN

ISRAEL

PART I

In the Shadow of the Great War

# CHAPTER ONE

## AFTER THE WAR

Armistice Day, 1928. In the crowded streets of an English city there is a slowing of people and vehicles. A maroon sounds. Traffic and talk, all movement and noise cease. A small boy looks up at his mother's face in the silence. He wonders why she looks suddenly so grave.

The child was myself. The routine of the day had been interrupted by two minutes of silence to remember the dead of the Great War which had ended precisely at that time, on that day, ten years before. Those millions who had lost their lives directly in its course maintained still an influence on those who had survived. When I asked my mother why we had to stand still and quietly, she explained in simple words. I heard what she said but I did not comprehend it. Even in later years, when the maroon sounded and the world, as it seemed, came briefly to a halt, it struck me, a schoolboy, as merely an adult ritual. My adolescent judgement of the war, formed from the novels and historical accounts, the movies and plays which reflected it, was that it had been on the whole an exciting event. It did not affect my ideas or spirit any more than the stories of the battles between good men and bad in the old Wild West except that I could hear about the war from participants. I envied their experience.

Looking back upon those years in which I grew up between the wars, I see now that that experience accounted for so much of what was happening around me. The survivors' vow to remember the dead – 'at the going down of the sun and in the morning, we will remember them', declaimed on Armistice Day – was interwoven with another phrase, 'a land fit for heroes to live in'. There was an expectancy of a good life in those areas where, before, it had been mean or impoverished. That was why, among other things, at the going down of the sun and in the morning the dead should be

1

remembered. It was not only that the 'fallen' had lost their lives prematurely but that they had lost the opportunity to come back to happier times.

The returning German sailors and soldiers did not take up the phrase 'a land fit for heroes to live in' to describe their expectations of the fatherland but were quick to subscribe to a notion sown by political activists: the war had not been 'lost' by the armed forces but by corruption at home. In broad terms, the hard Right accused Socialist politicians and Communists in the factories – even within the very ranks of the armed forces – of seeking to exploit the circumstances of war for their own ends. The far Left blamed the capitalist system, citing *inter alia* the huge profits made by war manufacturers and entrepreneurs. The first of a long-running series of clashes between armed bands of these factions began on the streets of city and town, spilling into the countryside almost immediately. But for a time the majority of the German people suspended judgement on the political course they wished to follow. Though there was a widespread sense of national humiliation – exacerbated by foreign troops in occupation of German soil, the removal of German assets, the demands of the European allies for cash from their treasury – most immediately and importantly after the war, they had a living to earn. It took Germans a little longer than the Americans, British or French to enjoy the post-war boom but, much helped by loans from the United States,* they became a part of it.

'We are apparently finished and done with economic cycles as we have known them,' the president of the New York Stock Exchange remarked in September 1929. He was not of this opinion just because the dealings in stocks and shares, the business of banks, was progressing so well. In Europe, and still more in the United States, the manufacturing industries were producing a huge range of goods at economic prices in response to rising popular demand. Yet a devastating financial crash was but a few weeks away, bringing ruination to magnates, managers, white- and blue-collar workers and pensioners.

---

* Between 1924 and 1930, Germany borrowed $7 billion, principally from the United States, the remainder mainly from Britain. Though she paid out about two-thirds of this sum in reparations, she was able to use the remainder for economic recovery. Unemployment fell from over 3 million in 1920 to 650,000 in 1928. Output in 1923 was 55 per cent of that in 1913, in 1927 it was 122 per cent.

2

This economic collapse and the depression which inevitably followed have become a bench-mark. After this, it is said, governments of the democracies tended to be timid: grossly subordinating foreign policy to advantage in currency and trade, inwardly apprehensive of popular unrest inspired or encouraged by Communists, constrained by the huge sums required to keep the millions of unemployed from starvation. No doubt some of this is true, but many of the defects in government attributed to the collapse and depression were perceptible in the preceding years of boom.

The United States, for example, made a popular choice to isolate itself from the international intrigues and alliances of Europe. The Senate declined to ratify the president's commitment to the League of Nations and thus nullified the Anglo-American guarantee of France's frontiers. It protected its industries from international competition by tariffs before the economic crisis and reinforced these afterwards.

War expenditure had made a short-term debtor of Great Britain. Its return to peacetime trading was sluggish and its unemployment remained stubbornly high during the ten years after the war, despite the endeavours of its first Labour government. Struggling to resume status as a world power in the economic as well as the political sense, it seemed to its own people to be staggering from one crisis to another, the quality of life falling from bad to worse. In fact, despite persistent deprivation among elements of its people, social security, health and education services were notably better than they had been before the war and were to continue to improve. The gap lay between popular expectations and their satisfaction.

France, too, was caught up politically and economically in recovery from the war. Her losses in manpower and her national expenditure had been greater than those of the United Kingdom. Huge tracts of her territory in the north had been laid waste. It is not surprising, therefore, that France, a notable victim of German aggression, should demand reparations as a means of assisting that recovery, not simply in manufacturing capacity but in the rebuilding of the many homes smashed by shellfire, the resuscitation of the cratered fields and the splintered woods. Among her people there remained a sense of unease, an apprehension that there might be a repetition of the events of 1914 and all that followed unless clear and binding political arrangements were made to prevent it.

Her former allies and late principal foe seemed to be in agreement that there should be such arrangements, not simply for France but for them all. The meetings between Britain, France, Germany, Belgium and Italy, the host nation at Locarno, led in 1925 to commitments to abstain from war as a means of settling international disputes, with guarantees that Britain would assist France or Germany if either of the latter should attack the other; and by France to assist Poland or Czechoslovakia if either of these states with whom she had special ties should be attacked by another power. Germany was then admitted to the League of Nations. In 1928, the Kellogg-Briand Pact seemed to bring the United States formally into the European agreement that war should finally be renounced.*

All this took place before the economic collapse of October 1929. What was not apparent then was that there were fundamental weaknesses in these arrangements. First, they did not apply to the whole of Europe – Russia, for example, was not a party to them. Then, the guarantees did not extend to the Middle or Far East. It could have been argued that the Middle East was effectively under the control of Britain and France but this was not true of the Far East. Japan was the rising power there, a member of the League of Nations but in no way vulnerable to the prime penalty open to the League when a member broke its covenant – economic sanctions. In Europe, the burden of such sanctions would fall upon Britain, a fact which successive British governments perceived only dimly and the British people saw not at all. But still, Britain held the responsibility. In the Pacific, the burden might have been assumed by the United States but the latter was neither a member of the League nor committed to any form of action if Japan should break the League's covenant.† The Kellogg-Briand Pact had only put nations on their honour to eschew war as a means of policy.

Overall, the former allies who worked so wholeheartedly to prevent the outbreak of a second world war were too much influenced by the experience of June and July 1914. They were so obsessed by the circumstances in which European nations

---

* The US, France, UK, Belgium, Italy, Japan, Poland and Czechoslovakia agreed to solve international disputes only 'by pacific means'. Germany was excluded because her forces were constrained by the Treaty of Versailles.
† The Washington Treaty of 1922 *inter alia* engaged the US, Belgium, British Empire, China, France, Italy, Japan, Netherlands and Portugal 'to respect the territorial integrity of China'.

4

'stumbled' into war, as Lloyd George later described it, in that summer that they tailored their measures to counter a recurrence of that nature. They were short on historical perspective. The object lesson of Napoleon's political aspirations and appetite was lost to them. They did not provide for the rise of another dictator who would pick off victims singly, counting on the short-sighted self-interest of neighbours to keep them out of the action. Though some recognised the economic dilemmas of Japan and the tenacious hold of militarism among its people, most forgot her successful surprise attack on the Tsar's fleet in Port Arthur two decades earlier.

All this is now plain. It was not so plain when the wounds of a terrible war were scarcely healed. The great majority of those who bore the fresh scars were not only anxious to avoid being wounded again; they could not believe that anyone else would readily revert to war as an instrument of policy.

Disarmament was not a requirement of the Locarno agreements any more than it was a part of the Kellogg-Briand Pact. The economic and emotional legacies of the First World War militated for it, however. The principle that the first duty of a nation state is to defend itself lost currency as a consequence. Among the democracies, those ministers responsible for the organisation and supply of national armed forces mostly found themselves the least favoured for public money.

The United States was one of those who restrained defence spending. The upthrust of military ideas from innovators in strategy or tactics was almost wholly ignored or suppressed in Washington. France did likewise; she abandoned all capability for strategic manoeuvre, believing that her frontiers would be preserved by defensive lines. The age of officers promoted to major and the higher ranks became progressively older. Britain actually reduced its defence spending in real terms through the second half of the 1920s at the prompting of Winston Churchill,* adopting the 'ten-year rule' whereby it was assumed at the beginning of each financial year that the country would not be at war during the decade ahead and would thus only need resources for imperial policing.

The financial collapse of 1929 inevitably led to further cuts in defence spending as revenues dropped and demands for subsistence

---

* He was then chancellor of the exchequer in the Conservative government of Stanley Baldwin.

increased among the mounting unemployed. As a result of these circumstances, the influence of the military in Germany was overtaken by that of Fascists under a demonic leadership, and in Japan the determination of the military to expand the empire by conquest was exalted. In less than a decade, internal elements opposed to the course of politico-military opportunism were made powerless or crushed; both nations rearmed and expanded their territory by threat or use of violence.

Year by year as these activities continued, the principle democracies looked on, taking no effective action to confront them. In Europe, the principal culprits were Great Britain and France. In the Far East, culpability lay with the United States. The governments of the time told themselves and others equally menaced by these events that their peoples would not tolerate any policy of intervention which might lead to war, forgetting perhaps that they had been elected to lead, not to follow. In Europe they persisted in this attitude even after the commonality began to perceive the recklessness of German power. The irresolution of the French government, the British practice of appeasement, had become so habitual that ministers and members of parliament were slow to see the growth of popular support for defence measures. In the United States, the mood of isolationism persisted beyond the outbreak of war in Europe, inhibiting the extension of its defensive strength. American reluctance to recognise that it might be attacked by Japan was bolstered by a belief that its people, principally occidental in origin, were as likely to prove superior to orientals on the battlefield as in every other activity.

The opening rounds of the Second World War in Europe were painful and debilitating, the more so because they demonstrated in the land battles that the power of the aggressors was irresistible. They raised serious doubts as to whether it would be possible for France and the British Empire to fight a holding action while mobilising the whole of their resources for a counter-offensive. When France fell, the British Isles might well have been invaded and conquered. The imperial forces in the Middle East would then have lost their prime source of supplies and reinforcement. The whole weight of German arms, aided by the output of British factories, might have been turned on the Soviet Union. When the war began in the Pacific, the major part of the United States carrier force escaped more by luck than judgement. Their loss at Pearl

Harbor would have seriously delayed the containment of Japan. Assuming that North America was unconquerable, and that Germany and Japan might ultimately have been defeated by a combination of residual forces under her leadership, what suffering, what outpouring of lives and treasure, would have been added to that actually involved in the years to 1945 before such a war came to an end.

Those perilous early years have now largely been forgotten by American participants and those in the British Commonwealth whose countries were not occupied. It is the later years, the years of victory, that are remembered. And the generations that have followed know almost nothing of them. There is a tendency to believe that victory is inevitable for those who are the victims of aggression. The British now think that they were bound to win in the Falklands in 1982 when in fact the outcome was in the balance until a late hour. Such ideas are misleading. They incline nations steeped in liberty to take their security for granted.

In contrast, the Soviet Union constantly reminds its citizens of the appalling losses and other suffering between 1941 and 1945 in what is termed the Great Patriotic War. It is state policy continuously to remind the war generation and to teach their successors that Russia fought the war in Europe almost single-handed because the Western allies hung back, hoping that, in having its forces torn to pieces on the Eastern Front, Germany would also destroy the Soviet apparatus. The reckless treatment of the Red Army, the misjudgements and machinations of Stalin and his henchmen which enfeebled Russia before the war, are conveniently forgotten or explained away. The Soviet Union's maintenance of huge armed forces is justified by the assertion that the Western democracies, fearing the philosophy of Communism, are forever seeking to overcome it by war.

Europe has now been at peace for more than forty years. It is far from surprising that many people among the democracies have lost sight of those years between the two world wars when vacillation, appeasement and isolationism flourished; when expenditure on defence was so constrained that it succeeded neither in deterring war nor, when war came, in providing an effective means of resisting aggression. The bitter years of defeat have passed into obscurity with time and so, too, has the anxious decade after 1945. Some rational folk among the democracies believe that because they have no wish to go to war with anybody, nobody will wish to go to war with them. It is a philosophy that suggests a need to disarm unilaterally, to be rid especially of nuclear weapons. Some think that NATO will protect them, whether it is funded properly or not. 'God takes care of the righteous.'

The following pages tell a cautionary tale. They recount the rise of militarism in Europe, the enhancement of it in the Far East after the First World War and the penalties paid by the powers who looked on as individual victims were preyed upon and brought down. The pointlessness of maintaining forces which are neither able to deter war nor to defend successfully against attack is illustrated by sketches of the first two campaigns in Europe – in Poland and in Norway – and in the Far East – in Malaya and the Philippines. Then it is recalled how, as soon as the victory over Germany and Japan was won, Stalin attempted to expand his power by force and violence in Europe and the way in which this was stemmed. And it is considered to what extent the democracies of the Atlantic Alliance are threatened still, are endangered still, by a war whose opening rounds might be lost if their political vigilance and popular will to defend themselves ebbed away once more.

# CHAPTER TWO

## 'THE ESSENTIAL ELEMENT OF POWER IS THE ABILITY TO APPLY FORCE,'

A peace treaty between the recently warring nations was drawn up at Versailles in June 1919 and ratified in 1920. Its terms did not impose disarmament on the new German Republic or restraint on her defence spending in the accepted meaning of those terms. Rather, it constrained her defence establishment.

A national army – the *Reichsheer* – would be permitted to police the borders of the state and to maintain order internally. To deny an accumulation of reserves, the force was to be composed of long-service volunteers, the officers engaging for a minimum of twenty-five years, the soldiers for a minimum of twelve. None of these were to be placed into any sort of reserve thereafter and no reserve was to be created from those who had formerly served in the old Imperial Army.* The absolute ceiling of combatants was 4,000 officers and 96,000 other ranks, whose numbers might be organised into a headquarters, seven infantry and three cavalry divisions, grouped as required in two corps or *Gruppenkommandos*. Within these field formations, there was to be no heavy artillery, no tanks, no aircraft and no capacity for using poisonous gas. The General Staff was to be disbanded and professional staff training ended. Similar conditions were drawn up for the creation of a small navy for coastal policing. Defence industries were to be constrained: one factory would be permitted for each principle requirement. The Krupps armaments complex was to be broken up.

These terms were dictated by the Allies after much debate among themselves, particularly between Britain and France, and grudgingly accepted by the German representatives; grudgingly and

---

* A further constraint on numbers was the 5 per cent ceiling placed on recruitment of replacements for those prematurely discharged or dying in any year.

uncertainly because they were unacceptable to the sizeable numbers in Germany who were opposed to any constraint in the recovery of national sovereignty. Foremost among these was the Officer Corps and, to an extent, the non-commissioned officers of the former Imperial Army.

Yet the Versailles Treaty was only one of a number of vexations current then in German political life. The 'revolutionary' government which had been put into power by Leftist mobs of workers, swollen by some of the returning sailors* and soldiers who had deserted as soon as they had returned to their home localities, was chiefly composed of Social Democrats. The most militant of the Communist revolutionary groups, the Spartacists, hoped soon to seize power in much the same way as workers and soldiers had done in Russia in 1917, when the Social Democrats under Kerensky had been ousted in favour of Lenin and the Communist Party. Bands of a revolutionary militia were forming in the final days of the war and multiplied rapidly immediately after the armistice in November 1918. Ministers of the new government were often unable to leave their offices, fearing with reason that extremists among the mobs outside might murder them. To restore order they turned necessarily to the army. This once great force was now a skeleton, its bones principally officers and non-commissioned officers. However, a number of right-wing groups had been formed illegally from ex-servicemen by an assortment of serving or former military leaders to counter the tyrannies of the left militia. They were known as *Freikorps*.

These were licensed temporarily and expanded to 400,000 by May 1919, sweeping away the Communists and radical Socialists, stabilising public order so that the civil police could resume their duties, and providing guards at all key points, not least for the National Parliament assembled at Weimar, to which the government had moved to escape the tensions in Berlin.

The *Freikorps* was a blunt but effective instrument. Irregular in numbers, organisation and equipment, it included men of criminal disposition. Most, good or bad, were contemptuous of the left-of-centre government which authorised, paid and fed them. A climate developed for a right-wing revolution with a partiality for restoring

---

* Part of the fleet had mutinied on 4 November 1918. The army had marched back in formations from the Western Front.

the monarchy. The Treaty of Versailles with its constraints on the armed forces and bill of reparations, was a precipitant. But the Rightists were fragmented. The *putsch* attempted on 12 March 1920 was poorly co-ordinated – like others of a minor kind that followed it – and thus lacked the support of the *Freikorps* main body. It was opposed by moderate as well as militant labour organisations – there was a general strike – and no less importantly by sufficient numbers of the officers corps in or out of service. Isolated, the leaders and their followers dispersed after a few days.

The man now appointed to head the new German Army was Major-General Hans von Seeckt. He was somewhat surprised as he had just resigned as director of the staff in the Army General Headquarters, the *Heeresleitung*, having declined at a dramatic midnight meeting with the minister for war on 13 March to give orders to shoot down the right-wing mutineers. He had previously been passed over as commander-in-chief. But the incumbent chief was now politically compromised and the advice of the few senior officers sympathetic to the Social Democrats was to appoint von Seeckt due to his outstanding ability and reputation.

For the next seven years, von Seeckt laboured to create a German Army which, while appearing to conform to the character of a limited security force, would be both a model of combat efficiency in the event of a need for operations – an *Eliteheer* – and simultaneously a cadre for expansion in case the opportunity should arise to return to general conscription – a *Führerheer*. Politically, his aim was to restore to the nation – as distinct from the government of Social Democrats – a capacity for power. 'The essential element of power is the ability to apply force,' he remarked on occasion to members of his staff. By this means, Germany would resume its place among the first rank of states. Without power, progress towards economic recovery and expansion would, in his view, be inhibited.

The first task was to restore the integrity of the officer corps. There were tens of thousands of applicants for commissions and thus many rejections. Some of those refused had been especially active in leadership among the *Freikorps* and departed embittered. Others were sought out and invited to rejoin. The criteria for acceptance were dedication to the army, rather than political party, in the service of the state; a reputation for honour, and for proven talent in arms and leadership, with a potential for responsibilities

11

beyond their present rank. It was not difficult to find officers with these qualifications from the great remnant of those commissioned into the Imperial Army up to 1914, and those with a similar background who had entered during the war.

Von Seeckt had already shaped one of the directorates within the *Heeresleitung* – the *Truppenamt* – to operate as a General Staff. Its members were set to work to organise and train an army capable of a mobile offensive strategy – a very different concept from that provided by the Treaty of Versailles. The selection of the non-commissioned officers and soldiers followed generally on the lines of the officers: no soldier was enlisted who lacked the qualities of a leader. A number of young men who had been at school during the war were also encouraged to join to ensure long-term continuity. Much care was given to the basic training of these recruits and to continuation training of the whole. A three-year cycle was introduced which provided commanding officers with ample time to carry through programmes of individual development in a wide range of subjects – weapons and equipment team training, platoon, company and battalion exercises – before involvement in higher manoeuvres. Progressively, there was a relaxation of the more severe and formal discipline imposed in the pre-war Imperial Army. Life in the trenches had already broken some of the traditional barriers between officers and other ranks. There was no attempt to re-erect them; regimental officers were advised to shift the emphasis towards self-discipline based on the expectation that each man would do his best as a matter of pride. Pay was improved – necessarily, the former conscript's pay had been derisory. Once qualified as a trained soldier, a man was assured of regular leave, was released from the obligation to sleep in barracks and from attendance at petty administrative parades. With slow promotion in an army full of experienced non-commissioned officers, special advanced-proficiency grades – with further increments in pay – were introduced for private soldiers.

The *Reichsheer* was thus an army manifest and an army hidden: that authorised by the makers of the peace treaty and that conceived by von Seeckt; the internal and frontier security force, and the force to be capable of a mobile strategic offensive. Within the former, the *Truppenamt* was able to develop professional expertise in such matters as co-operation between the fighting and supporting arms, the infantry and cavalry, the artillery and engineers; and to advance prodigiously the technology and practice of military comunications. Von Seeckt himself conceived the idea of staff and signal exercises in which only headquarters and signal units took the field to practise what is now called 'C3' – command, control and communications. In secret the army established armament-research establishments, sometimes in collaboration with private industry, and experimented in Russia – to the mutual benefit of itself and the Red Army – with tanks, heavy artillery and aircraft.

Von Seeckt was not, however, a military innovator. He did not conceive of great changes from massed infantry to an armoured mass. His aim was to restore the army's capability to what it had been before the First World War; the sort of marching field force which von Moltke the elder had committed against France in 1870, though one which made use of advances in weapons technology and the inception of aircraft. In this he had to combat the ideas of those who believed that technology was serving to consolidate the strength of defensive warfare. Such ideas were thrust aside. So, equally, were those which sought to advance too far in modernisation. To the suggestion that the bicycles of reconnaissance troops should be replaced by motorcycles, he responded, 'Please, if we are to remain friends, let us hear no more of such notions!' Despite these contradictions, the army developed its professional skills during six years of training.

While exhorting officers and men to remain outside politics – the soldiers in any case had no vote – von Seeckt had a political ambition of his own: he wished to become president of the Republic, though whether this was principally to enjoy the supreme politico-military authority invested in the post or to satisfy wider aspirations is a matter of judgement. He was biding his time when the Social Democrat then in office, Friedrich Ebert, died unexpectedly in 1925 to be replaced by the aged Field Marshal von Hindenburg, popular amongst all political elements but the Left and venerated by the army. Then, in an act of political misjudgement in the following year, von Seeckt asked the son of the former Imperial Crown Prince, Prince William of Prussia, to attend the annual army manoeuvres without the permission of president or government. He was obliged to resign.

Almost forty years later, General Student, who had served under von Seeckt as a captain, remarked that 'After von Seeckt we had chiefs we might like better, or who may even have been better soldiers, but none who had our absolute respect as he did and commanded absolutely our obedience.'*

For another seven years, under chiefs sympathetic to his ideas, the army continued along the course von Seeckt had laid out for it. Aloof from politics, it contributed to political stability as Germany passed through the grim years of financial crash and economic depression, as unemployment rose to six million. Aloof, that is to say, in its general conduct and philosophy but not immune to the political events and other influences manifest in national life.

The extreme Left in Germany continued to be a considerable force. In the parliamentary elections of 1928 the Communist Party obtained 3,265,000 votes, which gave them 54 (of 491) seats in the *Reichstag*. Two years later, their vote had risen to 4,592,000 and their seats to 77. Left-wing Socialists and Communists had an extensive propaganda organisation, particularly strong among factory workers and students. The Left-orientated *Eisner Front*† was able to bring several hundred thousand men out on to the streets from the socialist *Reichsbanner* and the Communist Red Front organisations when clashes with employers, the police or, more frequently, the Right, were considered politic.

In the *Reichstag* the Left element formed with the moderate Social Democrats a loose alliance of 220 members after the 1930 election. Seven centre parties had a total of 198 seats. The most spectacular change lay in the rise among the parties of the Right in which Adolf Hitler's National Socialist German Workers' Party – the Nazis – having polled 810,000 votes in 1928 to gain 12 seats had two years later secured 6,409,000 votes and 107 members elected, a triumph for the party's extended organisation, recruitment and propaganda. The Nazis had by this time a private army, the *Sturmabteilungen* (storm troops) or 'Brownshirts', numbering several hundred thousand men ready for concerted action with the older force of the Right, the *Stahlhelm* (steel helmet) organisation.

---

* However, General Groener, previously chief of the army and intermittently defence minister to 1932, wrote in 1937, 'I knew Seeckt as no one else did, and I always got on with him, because, in spite of the many shadowy sides of his character, he had a clear and clever head...But the best thing about him was his silences on which his fame was based...In difficult situations Seeckt was in no way courageous – he just lapsed into silence.'
† Political faction named after Kurt Eisner who had been assassinated while leading the 'People's State' of Bavaria, established in the political ferment after the Armistice in 1918.

Extreme Left and Right advances had been at the expense of the moderate and centre parties. As this polarisation continued, clashes between the private armies became more frequent. But the Nazi Brownshirts were better organised and trained and by 1932 more numerous; they had then over 400,000 men with a full range of light weapons and equipment.

Despite contrary instructions, individuals in the *Reichsheer* had not altogether disengaged themselves from political sympathies. Some, chiefly the more junior ranks, had been sympathetic to the Social Democrats but the continual attacks on the army by its parliamentarians and others had discouraged them. Among the officers, notably those most politically ignorant, there had been a drift towards the Nazis, accentuated as the middle and junior ranks saw that promotion tended to be given to officers with origins in the great regiments of the Imperial Army, notwithstanding all that had been said about professionalism being the criterion for selection. Yet even some of the most senior officers became convinced that Germany's difficulties would be solved best by the National Socialist Party.

Absolute leader of the Nazis, Adolf Hitler was urged by his impatient Brownshirt commanders to let them seize power for him by *coup d'état*. However, he preferred to wait, believing, despite many anxieties and uncertainties, that there would be a reward for his electoral success. As he had judged, the scheming of the Centrists and an element among the military leadership brought matters to the point where he was summoned to the presidential residence to accept instructions from Hindenberg to head a coalition government as chancellor.

# CHAPTER THREE

## A MARTIAL STATE

The new coalition government of National Socialists and Conservatives was appointed about noon on 30 January 1933. It had 247 seats of the 583 in the *Reichstag* and was expected therefore to proceed not only on the basis of consensus within itself but also some understanding with the centre party, which had 70 seats. Such an arrangement was intolerable to a man of Hitler's character, and even if he had decided to govern by this means it seems unlikely that his party, dedicated to political violence and excited by the sight and scent of prey, would have held together. The restraint he exercised immediately was simply to preserve some show of legitimacy in acquiring national ascendancy.

As the Centrists were unwilling to give him unqualified parliamentary support, he was soon able to persuade both them and his coalition partners that new elections were necessary. He had contrived successfully to appoint his own men in authority over the greater part of the police force,* and in the government information services. He secured the support of the principal institutions of finance and commerce by promises of favourable trading circumstances. 'Private enterprise', he remarked to a closed meeting with bankers and industrialists, 'cannot be maintained in the age of democracy: it is conceivable only if the people have a sound idea of authority and personality.' They knew what he meant by that.

The month of electioneering to polling day on 5 March 1933 is now infamous for coercion and terror. The main target of Brownshirt gangs was, of course, the Left of all shades: Communist meetings were forbidden, party publications suspended, and this

---

* There was no federal police force in the German Empire or the Republic which succeeded it; police were organised by the constituent states. Göring, as minister–president of Prussia, became head of the Prussian Police. Nazi sympathisers were in key police posts elsewhere.

was progressively extended to the Socialists. Social Democrat rallies were attacked, supporters beaten up, venues continually shifted at the last moment by the police on the grounds of maintaining public order. Intimidation extended to the centre parties. All the while, using government and party agencies, Josef Goebbels, the Nazis' chief propagandist, flooded the public with the message that Adolf Hitler and his National Socialist policies alone would restore Germany's prosperity and standing in the world. They alone would root out the internal agents of the international conspiracy against the nation – the Jews and the Communists. The public was warned that the latter would be launching a revolution at any moment.

Having done their utmost to provoke it, the Nazi hierarchy were vexed when the Communists failed to rise. Under Göring's direction, Brownshirts secretly set fire to the *Reichstag*, their propaganda organisation at once broadcasting that this was an act of 'Red terror'. Five members of the Communist Party were arraigned, somewhat unconvincingly, as the arsonists.* However, the ruse persuaded the president at the end of February to suspend those sections of the constitution which guaranteed personal and civil liberties.

Even so, the election validated Lincoln's dictum that you cannot fool all the people all the time. The Nazis increased their vote to 17,277,180 on 5 March but raised their share of the total to only 44 per cent. The centre party and Social Democrats held their positions with small variations up and down. The Communists lost a million votes yet still polled almost five million. Although Hitler's coalition now had 340 seats in the *Reichstag*, a majority of sixteen, he had looked for the two-thirds majority needed to change the constitution. For it was his plan to pass an 'enabling' act, whereby Parliament would effectively transfer its powers to the government in office for four years. Once more, many of his immediate associates urged Hitler to seize power on the understanding that the army and navy would not obstruct Brownshirt intervention, but he

---

* One of these was Ernst Torgler, leader of the Communists in the *Reichstag*, three were Bulgarians. The least influential was a fellow Communist, Marinus van der Lubbe, a mentally retarded Dutchman with a record of arson who was an unwitting tool of the *Sturmabteilungen*. He undoubtedly lit a few small fires, but the main blaze was kindled by quantities of petrol and chemicals too great for one man to carry. The evidence against Torgler and the Bulgarians was so flimsy that they were released. Van der Lubbe was found guilty and put to death by decapitation.

chose still the appearance of legitimacy. In the latter part of March, by an act of military pageantry, by the exclusion of the 81 Communist members, giving false promises and using a variety of threats, the *Reichstag* passed to the government for four years the power of legislation, including the raising of finance, the approval of treaties with foreign powers and the power to introduce laws which might deviate from the constitution. The voting was 441 for, 84 – the Social Democrats – against.

By this means, absolute power passed to Hitler within six months. As the only 'king' on the draughts board, he then took almost all the other pieces of the state in a series of free-running moves. Among these were the *Reichswehr*, the navy and, predominantly, the army. Their oath of loyalty was to the president as commander-in-chief; and though Hindenburg, the renowned *Generalfeldmarschall*, was not then so widely venerated as once he had been, he was still preferable to Hitler, the former corporal, as a focus of fealty to many soldiers. From his point of view, Hitler needed the defence forces; he would not have disagreed with von Seeckt's view that Germany would regain international respect only by possessing military strength. He may also have begun to sense that he might need the army, amongst whose members he was progressively acquiring a sympathetic following, as a counterbalance to the power of the Brownshirts. For their part, as Sir John Wheeler-Bennett has remarked, the generals

> ...wished to secure for the benefit of the *Reichswehr* all that could be gained to advantage from the Nazi movement, while dominating and controlling its policy. They were still dreaming in their blindness of a martial state in which the masses, galvanised and inspired by National Socialism, would be directed and disciplined by the army...

The chancellor, *Führer* (leader) of the National Socialists, began to encourage those dreams.

In the summer of the following year, persuaded by Herman Göring and Heinrich Himmler among his close associates that the leaders of the Brownshirts were planning to overthrow him, Hitler agreed to their 'elimination', and with them other political enemies, including two generals. It was only the deaths of the latter which shocked the army leadership. Otherwise, they were pleased to see the overthrow of the *Sturmabteilungen* which, armed and organised as a military body and more numerous than the *Reichswehr*, threatened their status. The fact that these murders were carried out by a new paramilitary body, the black-shirted SS (*Schutzstaffel*) – Hitler's personal bodyguard under Himmler's command – seems to have been unobjectionable as their numbers were so small.

Then, on 2 August 1934, Hindenburg died. He was almost eighty-seven. It was anticipated that there would be a general election of his successor but, three hours later, the government announced that on the basis of a law passed by the Cabinet on the previous day, the officers of president and chancellor were to be combined, the title of president being abandoned. Hitler immediately assumed the titles of *Führer* and *Reichskanzler*. Every member of the *Reichswehr* was now obliged to take this oath:

> I swear by God this sacred oath, that I will render unconditional obedience to Adolf Hitler, the *Führer* of the German *Reich* and supreme commander of the armed forces, and will be ready as a brave soldier to risk my life at any time for this oath.

The last knot was thereby tied in the political binding of the army and navy.

# CHAPTER FOUR

# REICHSWEHR TO WEHRMACHT

Five years lay between Hitler's assumption of unrestrained internal power and the opening of the Second World War. Whether the advance to that event is seen as a series of deliberately calculated steps – a planned progression from nonentity and failed revolutionary to conqueror of the occident – or the consequence of supreme opportunism, is a matter of choice. What is indisputable is that he transformed Germany's international standing and influence in those years from second to first class; in many respects to that of a superpower. This was accomplished principally by a huge expansion of the armed forces, financed by short-term economic measures, while asserting periodically that his aim was to preserve peace.

The expansion of the army and navy, together with the innovation of a separate military air force, the *Luftwaffe*, was begun as soon as Hitler became chancellor under Hindenburg. Additional recruitment was authorised confidentially. The lists of former officers of the army and navy which had been prepared in von Seeckt's time, despite the explicit instructions to the contrary in the Treaty of Versailles, were widely used and those individuals on them who were not drawn back into service were notified that they would be recalled to active military duty 'in a national emergency'. The intake of potential officers from high school was expanded. The budget for ships, aircraft, weapons, vehicles and equipment was doubled, comprehending notably the secret programmes which were procuring submarines and cruisers for the *Kriegsmarine*, tanks, heavy artillery and aircraft, and ammunition for these systems – all forbidden equally by the Treaty.

Having earlier leaked the news that Germany had formed the *Luftwaffe*, a matter well known to the military intelligence of most powers, Hitler suddenly announced on 16 March 1935 that he had reinstituted compulsory military service. All fit young men would be required to undertake one year of training with the colours, with a reserve liability thereafter.* The effect would be to provide the nation with half a million men under arms, sufficient to provide thirty-six army divisions, and additional complements for the new warships and air force,† though details concerning the latter two were not then disclosed.

The generals and admirals had not been given prior notice of this decision. Most heard of it on the radio or read about it in the newspapers next morning, a Sunday. The expansion was much greater than they had looked for and some believed it would take a decade and more to complete. All professional officers were none the less delighted. However much had been done under the counter to ease the constraints on a force ostensibly organised for frontier defence but dedicated to an offensive strategy, professional development had been inhibited. Now all constraints were to be removed.

In the following months, as each of the armed services extended its establishment, new barracks were built, new schools opened, the *Eliteheer* converted to a *Führerheer*. Among many problems was one of finding overnight sufficient officers and non-commissioned officers to provide for a tenfold expansion – a magnitude never conceived of by von Seeckt. As noted, many regular commissions were given to those on the reserve, but the numbers of those suitable in age and experience were marginal. Officers of the militarised police units and the border guards were recruited and selected non-commissioned officers commissioned. No doubt some of the latter should not have been; snobs, social and military, among the professional officer corps were soon making this criticism, but it was exaggerated. What was needed principally was a great number of lower ranking company officers to command and teach the conscripts. The former NCOs did this well. Enthusiastic, knowledgeable and hard-working, they enhanced close relationships with the young recruits by extension of contact beyond working hours – for example, having a drink with them in the

---

* Girls were not called to military service but were expected to undertake land or domestic work for one year in the service of the *Reich*.
† The cadre on which the *Luftwaffe* was formed was drawn from the army. A number of air and ground crews with war experience had been retained by von Seeckt.

evenings – without detriment to discipline or duty. They preserved the best ideas of leadership and training developed in the *Eliteheer*. Though their methods were arbitrary and justice was often rough, the system was more humane and productive than the perpetual bullying of the old Prussian tradition. The young men conscripted for service responded with goodwill; National Socialist propaganda apart, the nation was almost universally delighted that the Versailles shackles had been broken. Parents, relations, older friends exhorted young men to make the best of their service with the colours. They were received as young heroes among the civil populace.

The professional officers were also beneficiaries of the expansion. There was considerable promotion among the senior and middle rank officers, particularly those who were older and had war experience but for whom opportunities had been limited in the *Eliteheer*. Captains and below – and their equivalents in the *Kriegsmarine* – did not receive accelerated promotion; that was not in the German tradition. However, wider career opportunities were opened to them. For example, vacancies at the staff colleges and junior posts on the General Staff were increased.

Hitler was content to let the army, navy and air force get on with their work. His defence minister, General Werner von Blomberg, was sympathetic politically, very ready to remind officers that it was their duty to assist in the furtherance of party policies and standing. This included the weeding out of Jews among their number; the progressive reduction of religious teaching and observance, to be replaced by instruction in the party's theology; giving the party – later national – salute of the raised arm and '*Heil Hitler*' when on parade with party organisations; and adopting certain of the party emblems on their uniforms. The commander-in-chief of the army, who had been appointed at the insistence of President Hindenburg, was *Freiherr* von Fritsch, by no means Hitler's choice but to be trusted in so far as he was strongly opposed to any party of the Left and openly anti-Semitic. Though Fritsch remained in office after Hindenburg's death, his power as commander-in-chief was reduced by the insistence that Blomberg was to be chief of the *Wehrmacht*, that is, of all three armed services. On several occasions, Fritsch was to represent that this was contrary to Germany's tradition in which the army, as the largest and most important service, had primacy, and its chief was the principal military adviser to the head of state.

Hitler pointed out that, as things stood, the army in any case had prime place in its incumbency of the ministerial post and joint service command-in-chief, though he was careful not to say that it would be an army appointment in perpetuity. The issue remained a vexation to the upper echelon of the army but no more than that; they were busy doing purely soldiers' work and were reassured by the fulfilment of all Hitler's essential promises to them concerning the needs and integrity of their service. As noted, when the Brownshirt leader Roehm attempted to displace the army, Hitler frustrated him, a response which led to Roehm's estrangement and murder at a later date.

There was, moreover, a particular reason for brisk military expansion, Hitler informed his senior officers in February 1933 after only a month in office, and again in February 1934. The party had brought about full employment but this would only last for about eight years. After that, it would be necessary for an expanding population to find 'living space', a term comprehending resources and free markets elsewhere. The Western powers would resist this and it might be necessary consequently to undertake short, decisive actions to east and west. Some generals thought this merely political rhetoric; and all were agreed that the new large force would not be ready for war in eight years. Their clear advice on the disrupted condition of the services was ignored by Hitler when he withdrew from the League of Nations and the Geneva disarmament conference in October 1933, but may have dissuaded him from a serious blunder in 1934. On 25 July that year he inspired the murder of the Austrian chancellor, Dr Dollfuss, as a preliminary to union of the two German-speaking nations by *coup d'état*. But he backed away when his gunmen were overcome by prompt Austrian counter-measures and the Italian Fascist dictator, Benito Mussolini, gave indications of implacable dissent to this form of change in the character of the Austrian state.

A safer venture in as much as it was internal, though risking the wrath of the Versailles powers, was the reoccupation of the Rhineland by national military forces.* Planning began to this end in the spring of 1934, but Hitler had to wait for the moment when the risk could be minimised. By 1935, Mussolini was involved in the conquest of Abyssinia. The League of Nations was unable to

---

* The demilitarisation of the Rhineland was one of the measures by which France was to be reassured of security against attack by Germany.

stop it. The British and French foreign ministers proposed to do so by appeasement, which failed. In the United States, President Roosevelt proposed to the Congress that he should be authorised to ban arms exports to any belligerents (as one or more appeared aggressive), the decision being left to him as to the rectitude of Italy or Abyssinia. The chairman of the Foreign Relations Committee replied on 18 August 1935, that his colleagues,

> with few exceptions, were opposed to granting to the president the discretion of determining to which of the warring powers ammunition should be exported...In other words, the committee is almost unanimously opposed to determining in that way the aggressor.

Agreement was reached that both Italy and Abyssinia should be denied arms while the Congress was in recess. Mussolini properly took this to mean that the United States disapproved of his activities but was unwilling to involve itself beyond that expression. His representative in Washington advised him that the government was preoccupied with its programme of internal legislation.

Hitler drew much the same conclusion. It appeared that none of the democracies was prepared to risk war for matters which did not affect their own sovereignty. The question was, would any of the powers, particularly France, feel that that sovereignty was endangered by his insertion of soldiers along the German frontier on the Rhine? On balance, he decided they would not.

The announcement of German rearmament had moved France to negotiate a mutual assistance pact with Russia. On the pretext that this had weakened German security under the terms of the Locarno Treaty, Hitler launched three battalions into the Rhineland on 7 March 1936. His propaganda minister, Goebbels, saw to it that there was talk of the force being 35,000 strong. The German General Staff was acutely anxious. They feared French military intervention, and indeed thirteen French divisions were concentrated along the Rhineland frontier together with other defence measures. If any part of this force crossed to oppose the German soldiers entering from the opposite direction, the German plan was to withdraw. But Hitler's judgement – and nerve – was better than his generals' and the judgement and nerve of the French. The latter feared that the outcome of a clash must be a second world war.

With the British, they confined their reaction to protests at this 'surprise' action, though the French ambassador in Berlin had given warning some months before of Hitler's intention. The French also had, through excellent intelligence sources within the German Army, strong collateral to support the view. As the German people reacted delightedly to the successful assertion of national sovereignty, the generals and admirals had to admit that their predictions of failure had been false.

Two years later, Hitler decided on another act of lawlessness involving the armed forces. By this time he had grown impatient with both von Blomberg and von Fritsch. He was also becoming increasingly confident that the *Wehrmacht* as a body were personally loyal to him. The conscripts reporting for training, and their predecessors who had passed into the reserve, had been subjected to party propaganda over several years. Those who had been drawn early into pre-military training among the Hitler Youth movement had been exposed somewhat longer and elements of these had now become officers and non-commissioned officers in the reserve. Party influence had also been extended among the regular leadership. When Hitler held a conference on 5 November 1937, he again reverted to the real purpose of the *Wehrmacht*, a means of securing the territory of other nations for Germany. He spoke then of 1943 as being the year when expansion, reorganisation and re-equipment would be completed. After that, national, political, economic and military advantage might decline relative to other powers. It was clear to those listening that he was prepared to take these territories by military conquest if necessary while Germany's fortunes were rising.

Von Blomberg and von Fritsch spoke out against war with Britain and France. They advised that smaller states might not fall easily. The border defences of Czechoslovakia, for example, were strong; the frontiers guaranteed by France and Russia. Hitler made no response. But he was able to dispose shortly of all three principals at the meeting. Von Neurath, the foreign minister, was 'promoted' out of office to a token post. Von Blomberg, long a widower, made the error of marrying his young secretary whose past was unacceptable to the army. Von Fritsch saw to it that the field marshal retired but was then himself arraigned on a contrived charge of homosexual behaviour. He also resigned while awaiting the court hearing which cleared him but he was not then reinstated.

The army hierarchy had made the mistake of believing that they could frustrate or divert Hitler whenever it suited them. By the beginning of 1938 he held all the high trump cards: a centralised police and security service absolutely under his authority; a strong minority of party or personal supporters among the officers and non-commissioned officers; and complete control of the national press and radio.

The appointment of defence minister and its associated *Kriegsministerium* were abolished on 4 February 1938. A defence command, *Oberkommando der Wehrmacht* or OKW,* was established with the actual – as distinct from nominal – command vested in Hitler.[†] General Wilhelm Keitel, one of the old guard now subservient to Hitler, became chief of the OKW Staff. General Walther von Brauchitsch was appointed army commander-in-chief, his loyalties cemented by re-marriage to a woman who was devoted to Hitler and the party. The *Luftwaffe* was under Hermann Göring, a long-standing henchman now promoted to *Generalfeldmarschall*. The loyalty of the *Kriegsmarine* was assured under Admiral Erich Raeder. With these tools in his possession, Adolf Hitler returned to the issue of union with his homeland, Austria.

On 12 February 1938, the new Austrian chancellor, Kurt von Schuschnigg, was induced to cross into Bavaria to see Hitler at Berchtesgaden. From the moment of meeting, with the exception of an interval for luncheon, he was harangued and threatened by Hitler until he accepted terms which opened doors politically to the assumption of power by the Austrian National Socialist Party. Notably, the party leader in Austria was to be made minister of security in the government, while all constraints on party activities in Austria were to be abandoned. Apparently agreeing to these, von Schuschnigg returned to Vienna where he adopted an idea to draw national and international attention to what was happening. A plebiscite would be held on Sunday 13 March asking the Austrian people to vote on whether they wished their country to be 'a free, independent, social, Christian and united Austria – yes or no?'

The announcement of this plan was made on the evening of

---

* These letters were said by some army officers to stand for *oben kein Widerstand* – 'no resistance at the top'.

† On becoming head of state, Hitler had assumed nominal command as *Oberste Befehlshaber* (supreme commander). He now became *Oberbefehlshaber* (commander-in-chief), a lesser title but one connoting executive authority.

9 March. Despite the demands for *Anschluss* (union) by the rallies of the minority National Socialists in Austria, it seemed certain that the vote would be for continued independence. Hitler decided that the plebiscite must be prevented by a military occupation not later than Saturday the 10th. A bogus appeal was rigged from Vienna to Berlin – German forces were needed to help restore order in Austria – but the device was not needed. At the last moment, Schuschnigg gave way. Elements of the German Army, hastily launched from Bavaria, were already moving into Austria and Hitler's police and security chief, Heinrich Himmler, brought in huntsmen to run down every individual believed to be actively hostile to the *coup*.

It was as well for Germany that Austria did not fight on its frontiers. A third – perhaps as much as two-thirds – of the German Army's vehicles, armoured and otherwise, broke down along the roads to the border.

# CHAPTER FIVE

## 'PEACE IN OUR TIME'

Less than twenty years after the Armistice of November 1918, Germany was a state rearmed for an aggressive war to which it might be committed at any time by the decision of a single authority – the *Führer*. If Hitler had been tried by an international tribunal after 1945 he would have been able to point to the complicity of his accusers in defence of his breaches of the Treaty of Versailles and the consequences, at least to the end of 1938. There could be no denying that Britain and France, the powers that had a special responsibility, failed to exercise it; or that the United States hung back from intervention even when the dangers of German expansionism had become unmistakable.

Two factors at least appear to have militated in Hitler's favour during the years 1934–8. The first was the widespread dread among his neighbours of another war. The second was their own struggles for material prosperity.

At every point of crisis engendered by the Fascist dictators – Mussolini as well as Hitler – excuses were found to avoid the course of armed confrontation. The French believed that a counter-march of troops into the Rhineland to oppose Hitler's three battalions would lead immediately to war. Britain's response to Hitler's naval rearmament was to negotiate a bilateral agreement in which Germany's right to expand was recognised. Britain and France were also anxious to find any escape route to avoid military confrontation with Italy over Abyssinia and neither gave the Austrian chancellor the least support to encourage him to defy Hitler.

It was not that the non-German populace of western Europe was pacifist, though there were articulate minority peace movements among many nations. Rather, there was popular support for the pursuit of multilateral disarmament, though not at any price: the Peace Ballot organised in Britain in 1935 brought eleven and a half

million to vote. Eleven million favoured British membership of the
League of Nations and of these 6,784,368 believed that, 'if
necessary', their country should support military sanctions against
an aggressor, with 2,352,981 against. These sanctions were thought
of, however, as action to be taken by a British fleet – grey hulls
waiting below the horizon to fire if necessary – or bombing by the
Royal Air Force, as was undertaken from time to time against
rebellious tribesmen on the North-West Frontier of India.

Military sanctions were not, however, an option which politicians
of the principal parties were ready to adopt. Phrases in common use
expressed their outlook: 'No rational person wishes to go to war',
or, 'It is reasonable to assume that all nations wish to avoid the risk
of war.' The possibility that Hitler was neither a rational nor a
reasonable man was not seriously addressed. This may well have
been influenced by the fact that, the dread of war apart, the expense
of arming to match Hitler's potential challenge would threaten the
slow march to prosperity.

It has been a frequent accusation by anarchists and those on the
extreme Left that states whose economies are rooted in capitalism
are always ready for rearmament because it means big profits for
society's fat cats, including, directly or indirectly, government
ministers. The records of this century show that this has certainly
been untrue in the democracies. The absorption of funds and other
resources by defence departments in a phase of national armament
expansion is inevitably at the expense of social programmes and, in
the middle to long term, commercial growth. Ministers have
therefore resisted such measures whenever possible. Britain and
France were seeking throughout the period of Hitler's rise to power
to recover from the general economic effects of the First World War
and the particular impact of the financial crisis of 1929. The great
mass of French and British people were looking for jobs and a rising
standard of living, that 'land fit for heroes to live in' which they had
sighted and some had briefly enjoyed in the first post-war years.
The improvements which filtered through to those in employment
year by year understandably whetted their appetites for more. Any
change in economic policy which manifestly threatened the growth
of economic health would have been obnoxious to every constitu-
ency and, in the view of the more fanciful politicians, a stimulus for
revolution.

A third factor aiding Hitler internationally, arising from the dark side of human nature, was an element of sympathy for Mussolini's and, yet more, Hitler's philosophy and methods. In its most direct form, this was expressed by the small but militant Fascist parties organised in the democracies. Their influence was negligible. More persuasive were those who admired 'the grip Hitler has established over his economy' and the fact that Mussolini had succeeded in getting the trains to run on time in Italy. As the consequences of the Nazi programme became more evident, there were also expressions of support for its anti-Semitism.

These considerations worked similarly upon the people of the United States, struggling no less than Europeans for prosperity. When Franklin Roosevelt became president in March 1933, a third of the working people were unemployed. The New Deal which he had offered and which he carried through successfully for them was a huge task, yet by no means the only one which engaged him among internal policies.

In foreign relations, the United States could see problems on the horizon on two fronts: as an Atlantic power, Germany showed signs of becoming a menace to European security; but equally as a Pacific power there was anxiety about Japan's politico-military expansionism. Roosevelt was not helped by Cordell Hull, an upright but unenterprising secretary of state, or by a tendency among many senior State Department officials to believe that Communism – 'Bolshevism' was then the term – was a more important threat than Fascism. Among diplomats and magnates in commerce and the law there was also anti-Semitism. 'If we gave the Jews a chance here they would take us over financially and Hitler is afraid of just the same thing in Germany,' was typical of the advice they gave to the president in 1937. John Cudahy, a businessman appointed to head the American legation in Dublin, remarked to the State Department, 'The handling of the Jews by the present German government, which may be shocking and revolting, is from any realistic or logical approach, a purely domestic matter and none of our concern.' Ambassador William C. Bullitt regularly referred to Jews as 'kikes' and commenting on a Jew in the Russian government remarked, 'It is perhaps only natural that we should find members of that race more difficult to deal with than the Russians themselves.'

Slowly, as the demands of internal administration eased and a second term of office was entered, Roosevelt began to focus upon the threats to security. Aided by men such as Harold Ickes and Henry Morgenthau Jr, he came to see that the latter was right when he remarked in September 1938,

You know, Mr President, if we don't stop Hitler now he is going on down through the Black Sea, then what?... There is no question in my mind that if the countries in Europe would establish a blockade we could choke Germany to her knees and that is our last chance.

Yet the president was not an absolute sovereign. There was still a huge mood of isolationism in the United States, and not only among his political opponents. Roosevelt felt some of that same philosophy within himself. His inclination to overcome it had been set back in January 1938, when he had proposed confidentially to Neville Chamberlain, Baldwin's successor as prime minister in London, that he should host a conference for Britain, France, Germany and Italy to settle outstanding difficulties. Chamberlain, believing that he could restore Mussolini to international respectability – and responsibility – by appeasement over Abyssinia, declined American help. Another opportunity to intervene – to associate America with all its power in the braking if not the choking of Hitler and Mussolini – was not easy to find. Germany and Italy were involved in military assistance to the insurgent General Franco in Spain, but the anti-Bolsheviks were quick to remind Roosevelt that the Spanish government, markedly on the political Left, was receiving support from the Soviet Union. Hitler appeared to be threatening Czechoslovakia, but it was argued that this was simply to champion the cause of German minorities who were oppressed in that state.

Winston Churchill, out of government, proposed a 'grand alliance' of Britain, France and the Soviet Union – Stalin having offered to assist in the check of Hitler's ambitions – but Chamberlain saw no merit in the idea. 'You have only to look at the map,' he wrote to his sister on 20 March, 'to see that nothing that France or we could do could possibly save Czechoslovakia from being overrun by the Germans.' This ignored the option of threatening war upon Germany if they made such an invasion; the possibility of battle on two fronts could not have been undertaken lightly by Hitler. It may well be that Chamberlain rightly judged that the British – and French – people were not willing to make such a sacrifice. In September, as Hitler's public statements made it evident that he was intent upon military action, Roosevelt was similarly torn. Britain and France were being asked to agree to the Sudetenland – the territories with a substantial German-speaking populace – being ceded to Germany. Such a concession would shock America, the president told the British ambassador of 20 September, but 'he did not know what to do to help. If he disapproved of German aggression he might encourage Czechoslovakia to vain resistance.'

The Czechs were not so sure that resistance would be in vain. Russia had secured agreement to pass troops through Rumania to assist them, and the German Army high command had decided that a war in Czechoslovakia which involved sending troops simultaneously to cover France and perhaps Poland would certainly be lost. A plot had been prepared to arrest Hitler, Göring and Himmler, though whether the senior army officers involved would have acted is uncertain. However, France was mobilising and Stalin was ready to launch an army and tactical air force. As Hitler became anxious, Chamberlain saved the *Führer*'s reputation as a successful gambler.

The British prime minister's visit to Munich at the end of September gave Hitler almost all that he had asked for, not least an important sector of Czechoslovakia's frontier defences. As the French concurred, the Czech government had no option but to give way. Assured by Hitler that he had no further territorial claims in Europe, Chamberlain returned to London and spoke to the waiting crowds. 'I believe it is peace in our time.'

# PART II

---

# Baptisms of Fire

# CHAPTER SIX

## INTO BATTLE

As Hitler returned to Berlin from the negotiations with the British prime minister in Munich, he was heard to remark, 'That fellow (Chamberlain) has spoiled my entry into Prague.' This was not bravado. His tally of successes against all expectations from 1933 to 1938 – the accession to power by apparently constitutional means, the declaration of rearmament in 1934, the militarisation of the Rhineland in 1936, the seizure of Austria in 1937 – had fed Hitler's appetite for public triumphs. He had been looking forward confidently to driving through the streets of the Czechoslovakian capital. He was not going to deny himself this pleasure indefinitely. Ten days after signing the Munich agreement on 30 September, he wrote to General Keitel: 'What reinforcements are necessary in the present situation to break all resistance in Bohemia and Moravia...?'

He had not the slightest intention of honouring his agreement but retained a predilection for the appearances of consitutionality and, in the international arena, of diplomacy. Personal preference apart, these forms were useful in the strategy of picking off individual states, not least in leaving the timing of execution to him. A subservient priest, Father Tiso, had already been found to head Slovakia, the third great province of Czechoslovakia, as a German protectorate; Ruthenia was to be given to Hungary. Teschen, on the frontier with Poland,* was to be handed to the Poles. Bohemia and Moravia would also be 'protected', though somewhat more closely than Slovakia. Another campaign of political terror was embarked upon against the elected representatives of Czechoslovakia until, on 15 March 1939, its aged and demoralised president signed the following in Berlin:

---

* The district had been partitioned by plebiscite in 1920 as part of the post-war settlement of European boundaries.

...the aim of all efforts must be the safeguarding of calm, order and peace in this part of central Europe. The Czechoslovak president declares that, in order to serve this objective and to achieve ultimate pacification, he has confidently placed the fate of the Czech nation in the hands of the *Führer* of the German *Reich*...

That evening, Hitler drove through the streets of Prague, though the watching crowds were largely silent. His triumph was enhanced by the knowledge that the Czech military forces, some thirty-five divisions together with a tactical air force, were no longer a threat to his expansion in any direction; and the huge Skoda armaments complex, the third largest in Europe, had passed into his possession with the tanks, aircraft, artillery, ammunition and vehicles of the Czech defence forces. For good measure, he 'recovered' from Lithuania the district of Memel on 23 March, under threat of military force.

International reaction was varied. The Italian dictator, Mussolini, had been squared beforehand. The French protested hotly and began to consider a wide range of measures to recover from the blunder of trusting Hitler's word. The British began weakly – 'His Majesty's government have no desire to interfere unnecessarily in a matter with which other governments may be more directly concerned...' – but prime minister and foreign secretary were soon inspired by parliamentary and public reaction against this latest example of Hitler's wanton behaviour to abandon appeasement. The upshot was the formalisation in April of a treaty of mutual assistance between Britain and Poland; for Hitler's propaganda machine was already making menacing references to dissatisfaction with that state.

The treaty was signed on 6 April 1939. On the 16th, a note was presented in London from the Russian government proposing a triple alliance with Britain and France, joined by Poland if possible, to guarantee the integrity of those states in eastern and central Europe likely to become Hitler's victims. A difficulty for the British government was that certain of these states, notably Finland, Latvia, Estonia, Lithuania, Poland and Rumania, were as fearful of the consequences of a Soviet military presence within their territories as they were of the Germans. There were delays in responding. Secretly Stalin began to develop a parallel line of discussion with Berlin.

European events during the final months of 1938 and on through the spring of 1939 obliged President Roosevelt to consider inter-mittently the possibility that America might once again be drawn into a European war. It was not so much that the dangers of Japanese imperialism were receding whenever he raised his eyes to international horizons; rather that Hitler's persistent adventurism was progressively more obtrusive. His first offer of help during the approach to the Munich crisis having been rebuffed by Chamber-lain, he returned to the sidelines of the contest. The upsurge in Jewish persecution on the infamous *Kristalnacht*, 10 November 1938, when synagogues and other Jewish property were destroyed and a number of Jews murdered, horrified him. As a sign of his own and the American people's revulsion, he recalled his ambassa-dor from Berlin. But when Czechoslovakia was occupied and broken up he felt that something more than a token of disapproval was necessary, even though he was aware that isolationism was still the prevailing popular mood – a mood that extended to the exclusion of Jewish refugees fleeing from Nazi oppression. He deplored the Neutrality Act, telling Senator Tom Connally on 15 March, 'If Germany invades a country and declares war, we'll be on the side of Hitler by invoking the act. If we could get rid of the arms embargo it wouldn't be so bad.'

In mid-April he put to Hitler and Mussolini simultaneously the proposal that all international problems could be solved at the council table and urged them to guarantee not to undertake further aggression for ten 'or even twenty-five years, if we dare look that far ahead'.

'Are you willing to give assurance that your armed forces will not attack or invade the territory of the following independent nations?' The thirty-one states listed included Belgium, the Netherlands, Denmark, Lithuania, Latvia, Estonia, Poland, Finland, Russia, France, Britain and the Irish Republic.

Hitler and Mussolini affected to regard this message as trivial – 'Roosevelt is suffering from incipient mental disorder,' was Göring's comment – but each recognised that it required serious consideration. Hitler may have suspected Roosevelt's true intent: the illumination of the political crisis in Europe for the American people. At any rate, his response manifests the political skill which later events tend to obscure. He communicated with all those on the president's list with the exception of the three major states and Poland. Did they, he asked the governments individually, feel themselves in any way threatened by Germany? Had they authorised the president of the United States to put his question to Germany about their future security? Not everyone responded as Hitler would have wished, but the majority provided negative answers. Then Hitler made a speech to the *Reichstag* on 28 April 1939, with full arrangements for release of translated versions of the text abroad. He began by reviewing once more all that had befallen Germany since the imposition of the Treaty of Versailles, carrying this to the loss of territory in the 1920 settlement and referring to the free port of Danzig\* and the 'corridor' of land which had passed to Poland, separating East Prussia from the remainder of Germany. Accusations that he intended to attack Poland, Hitler remarked, were 'inventions of the international press'.

He turned to the message President Roosevelt had sent him, answering each point, directly or indirectly as it suited him, with a sort of comic seriousness. American freedom had not been achieved at the conference table. Germany had been treated at Versailles 'to greater degradations that can ever have been inflicted on the chiefs of the Sioux tribes'. He read out a list of the states asked by his Foreign Office whether they were apprehensive of attack by Germany. 'The reply was in all cases negative...' The list was so long that it distracted attention from the omission of states to whom the question had not been put, notably Poland. He reminded President Roosevelt that Syria could not reply because it was 'occupied', that Ireland was not oppressed by Germany but Britain; and that Palestine was having its 'liberty restricted by the most brutal resort to force' by British troops. He would certainly give an assurance that he was not preparing to attack the United States or any other countries on the American continent.

What Hitler did not say as he uttered this public rebuff to the president of the United States, was that he was preparing actively to attack Poland. On 3 April he had issued a directive under the codename 'Case White'. 'The present attitude of Poland requires

---

\* The old German merchant city of Danzig – now Gdansk – was removed from Germany in the frontier settlement post–1918 and passed, as a 'free' city, to the control of Poland. It contained a mixed German-Polish population.

... the initiation of military preparations to remove, if necessary, any threat from this direction forever.' The armed forces were to be ready to carry out the operation 'at any time from 1st September 1939, onward'.

Of course, these instructions may be read simply as precautions. Hitler's speech to the *Reichstag* impressed some in the international community as being reasonable, though those willing to take his remarks at face value were rapidly diminishing. But there were still remnant groups whose members felt that Germany had indeed been misused by the Treaty of Versailles and that she was understandably concerned for the wellbeing of Germans now living under alien governments. There were those to whom issues such as the deprivation of North American Indians, British oppression in Ireland, or the evils of colonial rule were so distracting that any reference to them tended to attract sympathy mutually, irrespective of the context in which it had been made. And there were the pacifists who held that what Hitler had done and seemed to threaten were wrong but that any military measures to counter him would be equally at fault.

It is doubtful if many Poles took this view. The Polish government and people were not going like lambs to the slaughter. They resisted the first phase of terrorisation. Germany was informed bluntly that any attempt to occupy the free city of Danzig by force would be counted as an act of war. Government and people drew strength from the support offered by Britain and France but, as noted, were uneasy about suggestions of reliance also on Russia. They were well aware that Stalin laid claims to those parts of the ancient kingdom of Poland which included some millions of Ukrainians and White Russians – though there was no anxiousness among these nationalities to return to the Soviet Union.

In their consideration of Stalin's proposals for partnership against Germany, the British government wavered and fumbled. The attitude of the minor Baltic states concerned put them in difficulties, but they multiplied these by failing to develop a clear and definite policy. The Russians, weighing the merits of alliance with the Western democracies as against those of Germany, were not impressed by the casual treatment of their negotiators by Britain, and did not find the latter's military potential persuasive. Long afterwards, Stalin recounted to Winston Churchill his ' "impression that the British and French governments were not resolved to go to war if Poland were attacked, but that they hoped the diplomatic line-up of Britain, France and Russia would deter Hitler. We were sure it would not."

' "How many divisions," Stalin had asked the British delegation, "will France send against Germany on mobilisation?" The answer was, "about a hundred." He then asked, "How many will England send?" The answer was, "Two, and two more later." "Ah, two, and two more later," Stalin had repeated. "Do you know," he asked, "how many divisions we shall have to put on the Russian front if we go to war with Germany?...More than three hundred." '

Stalin's reliance on the Red Army at that time is uncertain. It was not long since he had murdered 5,000 of its officers – believed, mostly on random suspicion, to be pro-German – and imprisoned thousands more. None the less, by 23 August 1939, he had become sufficiently pro-German himself to complete an agreement whereby Russia and Germany obligated themselves 'to desist from any act of violence, any aggressive action, and any attack on each other, either individually or jointly with other powers'. When this was made public, Britain and France were suddenly aware that they were alone the guarantors of Poland's frontiers, and in more senses than was immediately apparent: the price of Stalin's neutrality, kept secret for the time being, was the partition of Poland and the passing of Estonia and Latvia to Russia.

For Hitler, this agreement was crucial. His anxiety during the late stages of negotiation could not be concealed from his immediate subordinates, though his mood of aggressive confidence returned as soon as it was concluded. Three months earlier he had warned the heads of the military staffs that war would follow an attack upon Poland but had, perhaps, come to realise during a rambling *tour d'horizon* then, and intermittently thereafter, that this operation would be a failure if it drew in Russia as well as Britain and France. He had some doubts that the latter would fight if their guarantee was called in, so his resolve wobbled when Britain strengthened its commitment to Poland immediately after the Russo-German pact was announced. He was similarly rattled when Mussolini intimated that he would not fight immediately with Germany, and when the Japanese, with whom secret negotiations had been opened, broke talks off at this time. But the assurance that the Red Army would be neutral revived his belief that Poland would be defeated rapidly. After that he would, if necessary, turn the full weight of his forces against Britain and France.

Planning was now refined to include an act of gruesome verisimilitude. With political tension raised artificially by Hitler's speeches, the Poles would be accused of having raided the German radio station at Gleiwitz, close to the Polish frontier. Actors were cast for the play: a number of SS men, disguised as Polish soldiers, were to fire upon the station and manifest themselves to the local populace before withdrawing; a dozen or so inmates of a concentration camp, also clad in Polish uniforms, were then to be murdered by the *Gestapo* to provide bodies of 'raiders' apparently shot by German border guards during the incursion. International press correspondents were to be brought to Gleiwitz to see evidence of damage, hear accounts of the firing from the local populace and view the dead.*

With mobilisation and deployment completed, Hitler finally confirmed, on the afternoon of 31 August 1939, the date and time of attack: Friday 1 September at 04.45. Promptly at that hour, the Second World War began.

---

* On the day of the attack, 31 August, only one victim was used, but the SS men who carried out the supposed assault, also disguised in Polish uniforms, were later murdered to secure the secret of the deception.

# CHAPTER SEVEN

# MILITARY FACTORS

The German campaign in Poland continued until 6 October; in effect, for seven weeks. This short period does not suggest much of a resistance by the thirty-five divisions of the Polish Army and its air force, but that would be a false conclusion. The Poles fought bravely for their farmland and forests, their towns and cities. Their difficulty was not lack of courage but strategic and tactical weakness, compounded by antiquated arms and equipment.

Strategically, as defenders, they were obliged to deploy troops along their frontiers. Hitler's possession of Czechoslovakia had added to the length of these. East Prussia also had to be covered. Conversely, the choice of offensive lines lay with the aggressor. On these the German General Staff concentrated four armies: forty-four divisions and 2,000 aircraft. The northern group of two attacked from Pomerania and East Prussia; their *Panzer* (armoured) divisions combined in a single corps under General Heinz Guderian were to range widely to the east, separating the Polish forces covering East Prussia and disrupting their lines of communication. The southern group thrust from Silesia and Slovakia across the Carpathian mountains. Guderian's corps apart, all German forces were directed towards the capital, Warsaw, thereby pinching out a mass of Polish forces west of the river Vistula.

Tactically, the Germans had developed a system of simultaneous ground and air assault. The dive-bombers worked in the closest co-operation with the ground commanders from the outset, while medium bombers under fighter cover smashed the Polish air bases, attaining air supremacy in a few days. Thereafter, the *Luftwaffe* ranged freely, attacking ground targets deep in Poland but contributing also to interdiction, attacking Polish reserve forces and supplies moving forward to fortify hard-pressed areas of defence.

The six German *Panzer* and four light mechanised divisions among the four armies were equipped for the most part with light tanks, armed with machine-guns, but some were mounted with cannon ranging from 20 mm to 30 mm in calibre and a few with the short-barrelled 75 mm. Strength is a relative quality, however; as they were, these fighting vehicles outmatched and greatly outnumbered the Polish armour. Concentrations of the heavier Polish anti-tank guns were overcome either by direct fire from the tanks or by manoeuvre using the motorised infantry. All the German tanks had radios and the motorised infantry were controlled extensively by this means. The Polish armour – weak in numbers, scattered in small detachments – was largely directed by flag signals within companies. The chief element of manoeuvre was the horsed cavalry brigade, of which the Poles had eleven. Ground and air forces were not equipped for the new sort of war developed by Germany since the days of von Seeckt. The taxes paid by the Polish people for defence since 1918 had been largely wasted.

A further factor which assisted the German Army was its philosophy in leadership. Responsibility was devolved to as great an extent as possible. Junior officers and senior NCOs were expected to carry forward the task of their respective sub-unit or detachment, without regard for the decease of the appointed commander or loss of touch with the next higher headquarters, and to draw in remnants of other forces engaged in the accomplishment of the unit task. If circumstances denied continuance, the next senior man present was expected to do whatever he could to help the run of battle. Of course, in theory this is an expectation of the system of command in every army, but its application was inculcated within the German forces. Similarly, the ability of commanders and staffs in grouping and regrouping elements of different capabilities – infantry, armour, artillery, engineers – for tactical tasks as local circumstances required, long practised within the German Army, enhanced the potential of their mobile forces. The Polish Army employed a more rigid, hierarchical system of command and control and, although subordinates used their initiative in the progressively critical circumstances of defence, time was wasted while units waited for orders or were subject to frequent counter-orders. Their greater dependence on telephone communications exacerbated their difficulties.

Hitler came forward to see the fighting. On 5 September, he arrived at the headquarters of XIX *Panzer* Corps to the surprise of its commander, General Guderian.

> I met him near Plevno on the Tuchel–Swetch road, got into his car, and drove with him along the line of our previous advance. We passed the destroyed Polish artillery...Hitler asked me, 'Our dive bombers did that?' When I replied, 'No, our tanks!' he was plainly astonished.

This and other similar visits were an education for the *Führer* in the effectiveness of armour and air attack – he saw the Stuka dive bombers in action next day – filling out his ideas about modern warfare previously limited by his experience as a soldier on the Western Front in the First World War. He had been inclined to doubt some of the claims made by senior armoured and air force officers as to the potential of their particular weapons: he had been told that German air force assistance in Spain would hasten General Franco's victory but it had not seemed to do so notably; and he knew of the mechanical failures of the German armoured forces entering Austria. Now both arms were manifestly hastening what he termed 'the conquest of Poland'.

However, Hitler's forces were not engaged in quite that operation even though they had, by mid-September, drawn in almost all the Polish military forces. On the 16th, Russian troops concentrated along the 800 miles of frontier with Poland were told by their political officers that they were about to liberate the Polish workers.*

Next day, Soviet armoured forces crossed the frontier, driving towards the rivers Bug and San, roughly the line of partition with

---

* This was not the line revealed by the Russian foreign minister, Molotov, to the German ambassador in Moscow.

> ...the Soviet government intended to justify its procedure as follows: the Polish state had disintegrated and no longer existed; therefore all agreements with Poland (such as the Russo-Polish non-aggression pact) were void...the Soviet government considered itself obligated to intervene to protect its Ukrainian and White Russian brothers and make it possible for these unfortunate people to work in peace....The Soviet government unfortunately saw no possibility of any other motivation since the Soviet Union had heretofore not bothered about the plight of its minorities in Poland and had to justify abroad, in some way or other, its present intervention.

Germany; for Stalin had abandoned any idea of tolerating a 'residual Poland'. By 6 October, therefore, that state had ceased formally to exist except for a government in exile. Estonia and Lativia were to fall to Russian encroachment; Lithuania, which Hitler had expected to gain from the secret arrangements of the treaty of 23 August, was also gathered as a prize. Stalin sensed an advantage as the wary partners came to divide the campaign spoils: Hitler wanted to get his first-line troops out of Poland as soon as possible and was ready to make concessions to keep his eastern frontier peaceful.

For there was now a real threat to Germany on the western frontier. Not one conjured up by magnification of minor differences or specious argument. For the first time during his leadership of the German people, there was a possibility that his country might be invaded by powers of equal rank as a consequence of his adventures. A late attempt by Mussolini, whose political feet had become distinctly chilly, to organise a second Munich conference had failed. The British government, backed – driven, almost – by Parliament, would no longer accept fudge or compromise to escape from the commitment to Polish integrity. Hitler had persisted in the conquest of Poland and thus the United Kingdom had declared war on Germany on 3 September. Though reluctant at the last moment, France had done the same.

As the signs of this resolve became unmistakable at the end of August, Hitler was momentarily shaken, several times to the point of hysteria. When a Swedish intermediary told him that Britain would not come to an agreement because of a lack of confidence in his word, he struck his breast and cried, 'Idiots! Have I ever told a lie in my life?' There is little doubt that he saw and was momentarily daunted by the prospect of a gathering of enemies in armies determined on retribution; the situation which had once overtaken Napoleon – an end to the picking off singly of victims. But he soon recovered. A threat was also an opportunity to triumph yet again; a greater threat overcome would mean a greater triumph. In any case, there was no turning back. Germany's situation had been brought about by his policies and his alone. To admit their failure was not only alien to his nature but would involve his removal from power.

The British and French certainly made his continuance easier. On mobilisation, France had seventy-six divisions on the German frontier of which, the French chief of the General Staff had assured the Poles in May, thirty-five or more would be available to launch an immediate offensive into Germany in the event of an attack on Poland. Now the same chief told his government that it would be at least two years before an offensive could be opened, and even that assumed 'the help of British troops and American equipment'. The impending arrival of the four British regular divisions was not sufficient in his view to permit earlier action, even though the bulk and the strongest element of the German Army and Air Force was campaigning in Poland. The French were most anxious not to carry the air war into Germany in case this should lead to the bombing of French cities, a view with which the British government agreed in principle. So the Western Front remained quiet. Air operations were confined to reconnaissance and the dropping of political leaflets on German cities. It was only at sea that warfare developed. The menace of the submarine was quickly manifest.

If the Franco-British strategy was based on quiescence on land and in the air, it was certainly not Hitler's. Three days after the end in Poland, he prepared a memorandum which noted:

The German war aim is the final military despatch of the West, that is, the destruction of the power and ability of the Western powers ever again to be able to oppose the state consolidation and further development of the German people in Europe.

As far as the outside world is concerned, this eternal aim will have to undergo various propaganda adjustments...This does not alter the war aim. It is and remains the destruction of our Western enemies.

Russia would remain neutral for a time, he predicted.

In eight months, one year, or even several years, this may be altered. The trifling significance of treaties has been proved on all sides in recent years. The greatest safeguard against Russian attack lies...in a prompt demonstration of German strength.

The needs of the German economy and its vulnerability to air attack also dictated speed of settlement in the West. When the attack began, the same combination of mobile ground and air striking forces should be used. The axes should be through Luxembourg, Holland and Belgium, destroying the forces of these countries together with the Franco-British armies. With positions on the North Sea and Channel the *Luftwaffe* would be 'employed brutally' against the United Kingdom.

'The start cannot take place too early. In all circumstances (if at all possible), this autumn.' Hitler read this directive to his generals at Berchtesgaden on 10 October, immediately thereafter issuing a complementary operational directive. The breadth of the problems unsettled them, but more particularly they were made anxious by instructions to mount the offensive in the west in early November. The General and Air Staffs believed correctly that much greater strength would be needed to defeat the Allies in the west. That would take time to gather, not simply in the redeployment of divisions from east to west but in the disposal of weapons and equipment, vehicle and aircraft replacements and reinforcements, and in the expansion of the supply base – artillery ammunition expenditure in Poland, for example, had exceeded monthly production. Then, professional shortcomings exposed during the Polish campaign needed to be remedied.* All this would take them into the spring of 1940. The weather in the west would then be better suited to operations. In representing these views, von Brauchitsch once again failed his colleagues – some of whom were once more planning to depose the *Führer* – and, incidentally, finally lost Hitler's confidence. A more tactful and reasoned presentation of the difficulties by General Jodl of the OKW Staff may have been responsible for postponement of the offensive from one date to another through November and December, on the grounds of poor weather. Permission was granted for Christmas leave among the assembled striking forces.

Although the Western Front remained quiet, a new and unpleasant development in the east made Hitler uneasy in midwinter. On 30 November, Stalin attacked Finland, with whom Germany had longstanding ties. It was a reminder that Russia would use German reliance on its neutrality to the utmost. It also illuminated the Nordic dimension in the prosecution of the war.

On the afternoon of 10 October, the day on which Hitler had

---

* For example, the light division organisation had proved to be unsatisfactory.

read his memorandum on war aims to his senior officers, Admiral
Raeder reiterated the suggestion that naval bases should be secured
in Norway to assist in a submarine blockade of the United
Kingdom and concomitant relief of an Allied blockade of Germany.
A delicate point was whether Norway could be persuaded by
Germany, perhaps with pressure from Russia, to provide the
facilities which might lead to loss of her neutral status and
hostilities with Britain and France.* The OKW put a contrary
view. Almost half of German high-grade iron-ore imports came
from Sweden and between December and April each year, two and
a half million tons passed from Sweden through the Norwegian port
of Narvik, as pack-ice prevented transportation through the Gulf of
Bothnia. The ore ships sailed south through the Norwegian leads –
the inshore channels among the many coastal islands – ultimately
into Danish and Swedish territorial waters, until they arrived in the
Baltic. If Norway actively assisted Germany, the British Royal
Navy would not hesitate to attack this traffic in the Norwegian
zone.

The matter remained unresolved while the offensive in the west
occupied Hitler's attention. But with that postponed, and with
Stalin's attack on Finland, it re-emerged. There had been reports
from the naval attaché in Oslo that British landings in Norway were
imminent. There were many such rumours in the Norwegian
capital just then, fuelled by leaks of information from the
government machine. It became known that the British and French
were seeking permission to send troops and war supplies across
Norway to assist Finland. It was also rumoured, correctly, that the
Allies were seeking to persuade the Norwegian government to
permit mining of the leads to prevent the use of the channel to
bypass the North Sea open water minefields. In the second week of
December a former major in the Norwegian Army, who had later
been minister of defence, came to Berlin. His name was Vidkun
Quisling. Once a friend of the British, though already an admirer of
Russian Communism, he had turned finally to accept the tenets of
German National Socialism. He now assured Admiral Raeder that
there would be many Norwegians who would welcome a German

* A fortnight after the outbreak of war, the British government declared that an
attack on Norway by Germany would be treated as an attack on the United
Kingdom. The object was to encourage Norwegian co-operation in the naval
blockade of shipping and the extension of trade agreements.

occupation and consent to the removal of Jewish influences from government and commercial life. He was taken to see Hitler.

They met on 14, 16 and 18 December 1939. Despite warnings from the German ambassador in Oslo that Quisling's 'influence and prospects are...very slight', Hitler found him sufficiently impressive to make an immediate award of 200,000 gold marks to strengthen the tiny Norwegian National Socialist Party and its work against British interests. Further funding was promised. However, German preference, Quisling was told, was for strict Norwegian neutrality, but if the Allies should attempt landings they would be pre-empted. The OKW began to refine its ideas as to how pre-emption would be effected. The naval operations branch did not think much of these. It 'did *not* believe an imminent British occupation of Norway was probable' and reckoned that 'an occupation of Norway by Germany, even if no British action is to be feared, would be a dangerous undertaking...' These comments were passed to Hitler with the OKW document, 'Study North', in mid-January. He did not accept the conclusions of the naval staff and directed that there should be no further participation by that service's headquarters. The matter would be left to the OKW alone.* A strategic plan was to be developed and the principal planner would report directly to him. The project was to be entitled *Weserübung* – Exercise Weser.

---

* This was the first occasion that the *Oberkommando der Wehrmacht* undertook direct planning to the exclusion of the individual service commanders-in-chief and chiefs of staff.

# CHAPTER EIGHT

# WESERÜBUNG

Everyone knows where Norway is – more or less. In 1939, the British were inclined to think of Oslo, the capital, as lying a little to the east of Edinburgh, and of Norway looking indeed somewhat like Scotland. There were many Americans who, while recognising the distinctness of Danes, Swedes and Norwegians, would have been hard put to locate their states of origin in northern Europe. But the Germans were both central and, to an extent, northern Europeans. They had a land and sea boundary with Denmark. Sweden lay directly across the Baltic from northern Germany. The Norwegian leads had been important to them in the First World War as a means of bypassing the North Sea minefields laid by the British and Americans.

With the rise of Hitler, the German military intelligence service, the *Abwehr*, had surveyed comprehensively the physical and political geography of Norway, with its long coastline much indented by deep-water fjords. In the south its shores lie on the Skagerrak. For more than a thousand miles they ascend into the Arctic Circle along the North Sea, the Norwegian Sea with its western exits past Iceland into the Atlantic, and eastward along the Barents Sea to what was then the frontier with Finland at Petsamo. It is a land of great hills and mountains; an empty land. In 1939 it contained only three and a half million people. Its summers are short, the winters long and, in the north, spent mostly in total darkness.

From the opening of the war until the spring of 1940, the British Admiralty was concerned to close to Germany the North Sea exits, principally by laying a barrage of mines from Scotland to the edge of the three-mile limit of Norwegian territorial waters and, given political agreement, within these. When it became known that Germany was dependent on the Norwegian port of Narvik for iron-ore shipments in winter, the Admiralty pressed the British government to consider landing troops to prevent this commerce and the use of the railway from Sweden to forestall a German occupation. The case was put forcefully by Winston Churchill, as First Lord of the Admiralty, to his Cabinet colleagues. The advantages for naval and economic warfare were clear. So were the political problems of mining the coastal waters and occupying the territory of a friendly but determinedly neutral country such as Norway.

Stalin's attack on Finland, and the latter's appeal for help under the League of Nations' charter, stimulated the formation of a British military force to support the Finns, to which the French government agreed to contribute an equal number. There was secret agreement among the Allies that this opportunity might permit them to put troops into Norway to meet their earlier aim of blockading and pre-empting German movements. But the Norwegians showed no willingness to fall in with these ideas. The Allies could not bring themselves to violate Norwegian neutrality.

The Norwegians were themselves not above securing a double advantage politically. Whilst there had been long-standing goodwill for the Germans and respect for their efficiency in conducting trade, on balance their sympathies lay with the Anglo-French alliance. They derived comfort from the knowledge that their offshore waters would be protected by the Royal Navy. They chartered the bulk of their considerable merchant fleet to the Allies. They were assured by Britain's declaration that a German attack upon Norway would be treated as an attack upon herself. But they were not going to compromise their neutrality, to which they held both for political and moral reasons.* The small Royal Norwegian Navy with seven destroyers, four old coastal defence ships and two minelayers, was kept mobilised from September 1939. The northern brigade of the Norwegian Army was also fully manned, together with the naval and army air forces, seaplanes, eighteen reconnaissance and six fighter aircraft. Five coastal fortresses were also partially manned.

The Norwegians were unquestionably sympathetic to Finland under attack from Russia. A number of ministers and members of

---

* Norway and Denmark had been approached early in 1939 to conclude a non-aggression treaty with Germany. The Norwegians declined though the Danes accepted.

the *Storting* – the legislature – believed that passage should be permitted to British and French forces but the concomitant danger of a hostile German reaction was an irresistible counter-argument. As a compromise, British aircraft were accepted from Royal Air Force pilots at Sola airfield and flown on to Finland by Norwegians after an hour's instruction. The Swedes aided them *en route*. There were mishaps on take-off and landing as the Norwegian pilots picked up the characteristics of the machines they were ferrying. But all this came to an end in March when the Finns, who had waited four months for assistance, were obliged to accept Stalin's peace terms. With that, there was no longer an opportunity for Britain and France to gain a foothold in Norway under the cover of succouring a neighbour in distress.

By March also there had been a small but catalytic event in the war at sea. A German merchantman, the *Altmark*, had slipped into the Norwegian leads from the north Atlantic. Challenged by the Norwegian Navy, her master had produced papers which, with a glance round the decks, had satisfied the inspection party. But she had in her deep holds, in remote storerooms and even in an oil tank, 299 British seamen captured by a German raiding force in the south Atlantic. The Royal Navy was told to find the *Altmark* and, despite protest from the Norwegians locally, to board and search. HM destroyer *Cossack* caught her in Jøsing Fjord on 16 February 1940, released the seamen and disclosed to the Norwegians that this supposedly unarmed vessel also had aboard two light cannon and four machine-guns.

Even so, the Norwegian government protested vigorously. Their members were aware of the rumours that British landings might be tolerated by Norway. There were now rumours that Germany was herself preparing to mount some sort of pre-emptive operation.

The *Altmark* incident certainly vexed Hitler and persuaded him to advance his plans to occupy Norway and Denmark. On 20 February, he sent for General von Falkenhorst, a corps commander at Koblenz, who had had experience of winter warfare in Finland in 1918. Falkenhorst related at the Nuremberg trials that he was asked to speak about these but,

After a moment, the *Führer* interrupted me. He led me to a table covered with maps. 'I have a similar thing in mind, the occupation of Norway; because the *Reich* government has

52

information that the English [*sic*] intend to land there, and I want to be there before them.'

Then, marching up and down, he expounded to me his reasons. 'The occupation of Norway by the British would be a strategic turning movement which would lead them into the Baltic where we have neither troops nor fortifications. The success which we have gained in the east and which we are going to win in the west would be annihilated, because the enemy would find himself in a position to advance on Berlin and to break the backbone of our two fronts. In the second and third place, the conquest of Norway will ensure the liberty of movement of our fleet in the bay of Wilhelmshaven, and will protect our imports of Swedish ore... I appoint you to command the expedition.'

*Weserübung* was to comprise a simultaneous attack upon Denmark and Norway. The Norwegian operation was to be distinguished as *Weserübung Nord,* for which Falkenhorst was to have six divisions with strong air and naval support. He was sent off at noon with instructions to come back at 5 p.m. with his plans.

'I went out and bought a Baedeker travel guide in order to discover just what Norway was like... Then I went back to my hotel room and worked with this Baedeker. At 5 p.m. I went back to the *Führer.*' Falkenhorst proposed initially to capture the principal harbours – Oslo, Kristiansand, Stavanger, Bergen, Trondheim and Narvik – and the airfields of southern and central Norway. From these bases, his force would expand and converge, overcoming any opposition until the country was occupied.

It was now necessary to instruct the single service chiefs to provide the forces. Neither the army nor air force was pleased to find that an operational plan had been developed without their knowledge. 'Not a single word on this matter has been exchanged between the *Führer* and Brauchitsch,' the chief of the General Staff wrote in his diary on 26 February. 'That surely must be recorded for the history of the war!'

The announcement of the Russo-Finnish armistice on 12 March reduced Hitler's expectation of British landings in Norway – he had been told that an Anglo-French corps was in readiness in Scotland for the Scandinavian-Finnish venture. Would they now be acceptable to the Norwegians? If not, how could his own attack be justified? He fell into momentary uncertainty. Admiral Raedar did not help by voicing doubts about the viability of the sea expedition.

As noted, the British and French plans had been abandoned but the *Altmark* raid had led to a decision that the mine belt should be extended to the Norwegian shore south of Narvik. In case this should provoke a German attempt to occupy Norway, a British brigade would be sent into Narvik, with smaller forces going into Trondheim and Bergen. A raiding force would temporarily occupy Stavanger to destroy facilities, including Sola airfield. Some British ministers and senior naval officers, believing that the Norwegian coastal bases and airfields were essential to Allied strategy, hoped that Germany would overtly threaten Norway, precipitating the British response. The Foreign Office judged that there might be some local resistance, though not of a military kind. On reflection, scruples prevailed: if there was positive resistance from the Norwegian government and people, the landings would be cancelled. The mine-laying force set off from the Scapa anchorage north of Scotland on 4 April 1940.

Hitler had decided on 2 April that *Weserübung* should take place on the 9th at 5.15 a.m. Loading of merchant ships with troops and stores began at once. These were to precede the navy, posing as normal commerce, all troops and military equipment being hidden. Troops to be carried in warships were moved to Kiel, and those who were to land by parachute or aircraft closed in on the airfields of the 10th Air Corps round Hamburg. About 600 of the 1,008 serviceable aircraft in this formation were transports, the remainder fighters, dive-bombers – the *Stuka* – and medium bombers. One of the reasons why Denmark was to be occupied immediately was that its airfield at Aalborg in northern Jutland would be required for refuelling and rearming to maintain the intensity of air operations.

On 4 April, a member of the Norwegian embassy in Berlin, Ulrich Stang, was told by the Dutch military attaché that the Germans were preparing to attack Norway and Denmark imminently* though, strangely, the report of this to Oslo mentions only Denmark. On that same day, the *Daily Telegraph* in London reported that 400,000 German troops were ready in Baltic ports to attack Norway. These and other indications might have been

---

* The information was passed to the Dutch attaché, Major G.J. Sas, by *Oberst* Oster of the *Abwehr*. The leadership of this body was opposed to Hitler's war policies and passed information from time to time about plans and capabilities.

dismissed by the Norwegian government as another colourful batch of rumours, had there not also been, from 5 April onwards, reports sent by the Danish and Swedish chiefs of defence of troops embarking in the German Baltic ports and, subsequently, of these ships sailing westward through the narrows into the Kattegat. British submarines were also observing this traffic though, for reasons of security, they were unable to report the fact. Among them, the Polish submarine *Orzel*, in the Skagerrak, sank the *Rio de Janeiro*, a merchantman, off Lillesand in southern Norway on 8 April. German soldiers brought ashore by Norwegian fishermen said that they were *en route* to Bergen to save the Norwegians from a British occupation. This extraordinary news was sent to Oslo and reported to the *Storting* late that afternoon. Government and Parliament had just been made aware that British mines had been laid in the leads and the appearance of German forces, though coincidental, appeared to be the expected counter-measure.

The Norwegian Defence Staff now strongly advised the government to mobilise but ministers were reluctant to take any step which would, in their view, provoke Germany. There was time before the public broadcasting system closed on the night of 8 April to announce mobilisation, but the opportunity passed. At length agreement was given to a silent order: mobilisation notices were to be sent out by post. When the decision was passed by the defence minister, Colonel Rasmus Hatledal of the Defence Staff asked him, 'Are you mad?'

By now the German ambassador had appeared with an ultimatum that Norway should accept German protection against a British invasion of the country. He was instructed to wait in an ante-room while the Cabinet discussed their position. It was the early morning of 9 April. The German heavy cruiser *Blücher* was advancing up the Oslo Fjord, leading Group 5 of Falkenhorst's force on the capital. Ten miles to the south, the old fortress of Oscarsborg commanded a point where the sea passage narrows and the officer in command of the coastal batteries within, Colonel B.C. Eriksen, had been warned of their approach. Though he lacked instructions, he was clear as to his duty. The speed of the ships and the visibility were such that there would be time for one shot only from each of the three old 280 mm guns in the main armament. All fire was to be held until these fired. When the *Blücher* was within 1,800 metres he ordered engagement. Main and subsidiary guns opened, torpedoes were launched. The shells tore into the *Blücher* and she floated past, sinking. The pocket battleship, *Lützow*, was also damaged, together with several other vessels. These turned away to land their troops along the lower fjord.

News of this action reached Oslo shortly, with reports of other landings in Kristiansand, Bergen and Trondheim. The Norwegian foreign secretary gave a formal answer to the waiting German ambassador: 'We will not submit voluntarily; the struggle is already in progress.'

In the south, there was fog as the sun rose. In the North Sea a gale was developing. The first prevented the parachute assault of Forbnebu airfield at Oslo but it was captured a little later by a force landing in Ju 52 transports. Parachutists captured Sola airfield. Surprise, deception – some ships announced to Norwegian enquiries that they were British – and shock action carried the successes as far as Trondheim. Narvik fell about the same time after a brief fire fight by two of the old coastal defence ships and the threat of an intense bombardment of the town. Raeder's instructions had included the 'brutal breaking of resistance'.

In a matter of hours, life in Norway was dreadfully transformed. The Germans reinforced by sea and air all the centres they had captured. Offensive air squadrons were established in Norway and Denmark. Losses at sea of warships and stores ships and the considerable setback in the Oslo Fjord were all incidental to the process, however: where the Germans needed vehicles, they comandeered locally; fuel and food were taken at will. Whilst in many areas the invaders were initially few, there were no formed Norwegian units to oppose them. Nine companies, for example, captured Oslo by air landing, a city without a garrison. One of these, accompanied by the military attaché from the German embassy, pursued the king and government northwards. They were delayed by the bold intervention of a handful of the Royal Guard, some local unmobilised reservists and members of a civilian rifle club.

By 10 April, German reinforcements were arriving with light tanks, artillery, engineers and a range of support for the five divisions of infantry which had landed between the south and Trondheim. The 10th Air Corps had supremacy over land and sea. Aircrews were making up to three sorties a day.

The Norwegian Army gathering in the south was quickly overcome. The light forces of the navy were mostly shot out of the water while gallantly attacking German ships. Mobilisation stores, previously identified by the *Abwehr*, were widely captured.

During their pursuit by enemy ground and air forces, the king, with the agreement of his government, appointed General Otto Ruge to be commander-in-chief. His plan was to hold Trondelag, the region surrounding Trondheim, until reinforcements arrived to permit a counter-offensive to the south. For these additional forces he relied principally on the British.

# CHAPTER NINE

## 'ALTHOUGH WE HAVE BEEN COMPLETELY OUTWITTED...'

At 12.59 p.m. on Sunday 7 April 1940, British naval intelligence signalled the following to the commander-in-chief of the Home Fleet, Admiral Sir Charles Forbes:

> Recent reports suggest that a German expedition is being prepared. Hitler is reported from Copenhagen to have ordered the unostentatious movement of one division in ten ships by night to land at Narvik with simultaneous occupation of Jutland. Sweden to be left alone. Moderates said to be opposing the plan. Date given for arrival Narvik was 8th April...All these reports are of doubtful value and may well be only a further move in the war of nerves.

Air reports later in the day seemed to confirm that warships and merchantmen were moving northwards – they were Falkenhorst's Group 1, followed by Groups 2 and 4, *en route* to Narvik and intermediate ports. The element of the British Home Fleet at anchorage, the First Cruiser Squadron, was ordered to sea. Somewhat surprisingly, the troops embarked in readiness for landing in Norway in just such a contingency were hastily put ashore with what they could carry. The rest of their weapons and equipment remained on board.

Churchill and Admiral Sir Dudley Pound, the First Sea Lord, chief of the naval staff, were of the view that a naval action against the units of the German fleet 'undoubtedly making towards Narvik' must take precedence above pre-emptive British landings. Every available ship in the Home Fleet should join the operation in the North Sea 'to ensure that the German ships would not be able to return home' – as Mr Churchill informed the War Cabinet of 8 April. Submarines had been ordered to intercept stations. The

Admiralty believed that they would soon find the enemy. Unfortunately, with certain exceptions, arising as a matter of chance, the search was unsuccessful.

Cloud and sea conditions were unhelpful. The area of water was great. British and German ships narrowly missed one another on several occasions. The movement of the Royal Navy through the heaving waters would have been more purposeful if it had been co-ordinated with intensive air operation taking risks in the intermittently poor visibility. But they were not. Within forty-eight hours it was apparent that, while the British had satisfactorily mined Norwegian waters in the principal site, the Germans had captured those ports – and more – considered important to the control of the North Sea.

There was earnest discussion on the evening of 9 April and again on the 10th as to whether the British should now concentrate on the recapture of Narvik or attempt also to overcome the enemy in Trondheim and Bergen. News of the German naval strength in the harbours of both of the latter suggested that these would not easily be entered. 'We must seal up Bergen with a minefield,' Churchill wrote to the First Sea Lord on the 10th, 'and concentrate on Narvik... Narvik must be fought for. Although we have been completely outwitted, there is no reason to suppose that prolonged and serious fighting in this area will not impose a greater drain on the enemy than on ourselves.' In complement, joint plans were to be prepared to establish in central Norway 'a foothold by Allied forces at Namsos and Andalsnes', sites chosen from the map simply because they were geographically close to Trondheim. The offer of a French alpine division for Narvik, to be followed by another, had been gratefully accepted.

During the next few days the full extent of *Weserübung* became apparent. Denmark was lost;\* the whole of southern Norway occupied; and central Norway threatened. But the Allies were not inactive. At Narvik, Captain Warburton-Lee had led a force of destroyers into the fjord to destroy most of the German merchantmen there – most importantly the ammunition carrier *Rauenfels* – and reduce the warship strength by half, though at the cost of his

---

\*   *Weserübung Sud*, conducted under a separate commander and staff, completed the occupation of Denmark in a matter of hours. With frontiers open to Germany and Copenhagen occupied by surprise, the government decided that, with only a small defence force, resistance was pointless.

life. Attacks in the open sea favoured the British. Several squadrons of the Fleet Air Arm and the Royal Air Force had attacked airfields and warships. A German air raid on Scapa Flow had been destroyed in the air. The first troop convoy departed for Narvik. More troops were embarking.

Looking back, knowing so much about events, it is evident that much of this activity was misdirected. The British organisational arrangements for conducting operations of this kind were inadequate to meet the circumstances. A military co-ordinating committee had been established under Churchill as the senior of the three service ministers, though the prime minister took the chair from time to time and more frequently as operations proceeded. The chiefs of staff provided the military advice. But at the outset of a major war the committee had an enormous range of other matters to discuss, including preparations for countering an onslaught by Germany on the Western Front which they apprehended must be expected shortly. The political and military chiefs of the three services were also much concerned with pursuing their own needs, seeking as great a share of the manufacturing, technological and other resources as possible in developing the operational capability of their individual forces. A commander-in-chief should have been appointed immediately for the Norwegian venture with authority over the sea, land and air forces allocated. As it was, the Narvik force departed with separate naval and land commanders, each answerable to his service ministry. When, later, landing forces were sent to Namsos and Andalsnes, each was controlled directly by the War Office.

In London, the General Staff preparing the force assumed that they should follow arrangements for the earlier plan. But these involved troops lightly armed, lacking armour, anti-tank guns, adequate field or anti-aircraft guns and a balanced air component. What might have been sufficient for the occupation of Norwegian ports pre-emptively was insufficient for fighting the German Army for their possession. Without any good reason, the enemy was assumed also to be 'lightly armed' because they were known to be parachute troops and infantry. No notice was taken of firm information that German tanks had been in action from 10 April. The early reports that enemy numbers arriving in Norway were small persuaded some members of both the Joint Planning Staff and members of the Military Operations Directorate that they would remain small, even after several days of intelligence that sea and air movements of German forces into Norway were continuing.

There were other serious omissions: for example, an inexcusable ignorance about conditions in Norway. The fact that it was April suggested to those working in an English spring that most of the snow had gone, though the Norwegian embassy would have provided the information that there would still be snow in south Norway and deep snow in central and northern Norway. Cross-country movements without skis or snow shoes would be extremely limited.

The Royal Navy had also not yet come to recognise how vulnerable ships were to air attack; it was still believed by many senior naval officers that a warship had a high chance of survival provided it had a full fit of anti-aircraft weapons. The Royal Air Force hierarchy wanted to fight the war independently, only accepting a part in joint operations as a matter of indulgence. Air power, it was understood, was mobile and should thus be controlled at the highest level. Yet this mobility was not employed to support sea and land operations in Norway at the temporary expense of the currently inactive Western Front. The question was never posed: if air power is so decisive and the operations across the North Sea cannot be covered comprehensively from the air, is there any point in sending ships or troops?

Of course, resources were limited. Britain was rapidly attempting to make good the deficiencies of defence budgets under the rolling ten-year rule, and the times were perilous. But they were made more so by one or another form of blinkers worn by those from whom a breadth of vision was expected.

In contrast, General von Falkenhorst was well placed. He had a clear objective and authority* over the conduct of land and air operations. Although the German Navy was not under his command, he had only to ask for naval support and it was granted. Not unimportantly, he had the advantage of a small headquarters manned by a well-trained staff whose members expected to take wide responsibility, referring to a superior only when some matter arose which manifestly affected the realisation of the objective.

---

\* *Generaloberst* H-J. Stumpf, a former chief of staff of the *Luftwaffe*, commanded 10th Air Corps. He accepted instructions for support of the land battle. An important element of his staff was integrated for the operation with that of General von Falkenhorst.

They coped well in the early stages of the landings when communications were difficult, using *ad hoc* channels.

Falkenhorst could have done without Hitler's anxiety. The *Führer* showed signs of nose-diving when the early reports came in of losses at sea and the rate of expansion seemed slow. He was frequently worried about the exposure of the force at Narvik.

Three weeks after the landings, the German forces in the south had linked up with those at Trondheim. Their men in that city had been considerably outnumbered by the total of 13,000 British troops landed at Andalsnes and Namsos and the units of the Norwegian Army in the vicinity. Both sides were short of supporting weapons and vehicles. The snow restricted manoeuvre. A bold landing plan, Operation Hammer, launched swiftly would have threatened the German position in central Norway, but the risks it involved daunted the British chiefs of staff. The lack of central direction of their efforts, their own unfamiliarity in working closely together, the anxiety of the Air Staff that they were being drawn into an operation they would not control and late recognition by the Admiralty that ship losses might be high, all led to abandonment of the scheme. While they wavered, the German strength grew, notably in the extension of air attacks upon the force bases at Andalsnes and Namsos. Imperilled, the British forces were withdrawn at the beginning of May and with them ended General Ruge's prospect of stabilising the defence in Trondelag.

However, there were still British forces to the north in Mosjøen, Mo and Bodø, and a growing Allied strength in Narvik. The French alpine troops, made up to divisional strength by foreign legionaries and Poles, had joined the British in the area. British naval strength, augmented by Polish warships, denied Hitler any prospect of reinforcing – or rescuing – by sea the 2,000 members of *Generalleutnant* Eduard Dietl's Austrian mountain division landed by sea on 9 April. Anti-aircraft cruisers afloat and additional batteries ashore reduced the effects of German air attack. There had been, however, a difference of view between the naval and land commanders – the first ready to take risks, the second to avoid them. Opportunities had been missed. General Auchinleck was sent out to command the Allied forces remaining in Norway with a particular remit to take Narvik once and for all.

By the second half of May, a British brigade brought from the Western Front swelled the Allied land force numbers to more than

20,000. With the Norwegians in the area the total was close to 26,000. General Dietl had 1,800 sailors, the survivors of the destroyers defeated by Captain Warburton-Lee and a subsequent heavier naval attack. The 10th Air Corps had parachuted reinforcements to him at various intervals and others had come by courtesy of Sweden up the railway from Lulea – in all another 1,100, at most a total of 5,000. But this number was stretched holding the Narvik perimeter and the railway. It was the Germans' growing weakness from mid-April which caused Hitler to sit 'hunched in a chair in the corner...a picture of brooding gloom'. He contemplated withdrawing the force through Sweden but his staff, by one means and another, stifled his orders.

At last, on the night of 27/28 May, a comprehensive Allied attack was launched on Narvik: across water by two battalions of the Foreign Legion, a Norwegian battalion and a section of light tanks; overland by Polish and French troops – the *Chasseurs Alpins* – on skis, and by Norwegians under General Fleischer on skis and on foot. Naval gunfire joined the support of French, Norwegian and British batteries. Fighting for the final heights commanding Narvik was fierce but at last it fell. Preparations for the assault had been aided by Royal Air Force Hurricanes and Gladiators holding off German air attacks, but Bardufoss, their airfield to the north, was in fog on the 28 May while the skies to the south were clear. German dive-bombers appeared, concentrating on the Allied warships which, with the concurrence of the French general locally in command, withdrew.

So, too, did the Allied force within a few days. German troops were approaching from the south but, more decisively, the expected attack had been launched against France and Belgium. There was no possibility that Britain and France could maintain two fronts. The grim news had to be passed to the Norwegian government and General Ruge that Norway was to be abandoned.

The departure was well conducted under the arrangements of General Auchinleck and Admiral Lord Cork.* Deception was excellent and the Royal Air Force fighters continued in action until the last, finally landing on the carrier *Glorious*, though none of the pilots had ever put down on a carrier deck before. The anti-aircraft

---

\* Admiral of the Fleet, the Earl of Cork and Orrery, recalled from the reserve to assist Churchill in the Admiralty, had been in command of the naval force at Narvik from the outset of operations.

gunners remained also to the last hours, necessarily leaving much of their equipment behind, destroyed at the moment of abandonment. Royal Engineers cratered the runway at Bardufoss. The army passengers were carried safely home but a German naval sortie found the carrier *Glorious* and sank her with decks laden with the Royal Navy and Royal Air Force aircraft – a grievous loss of crew and pilots.

'Although we are outwitted...' – indeed, the British, French and Norwegians were, but that was the least of it. The opening rounds went to the Germans for an accumulation of reasons, all of which were characterised by the advantages of one nation deliberately attacking another with the benefit of surprise.

Norway was a country determined to remain neutral in the Second World War as she had in the First. Hitler's persistence in picking off European nations singly for subjection in one form or another in the Third *Reich* persuaded her government that it should increase its defence budget; but to little effect. Weapons and equipment to permit sustained defence were lacking. Training was inadequate: most Norwegian recruits completed only thirteen weeks of very elementary training before being returned to civil life. Their training in the reserve was deficient. Reserve units consisted of officers and men who had never served together – many had never even met – previously. No steps had been taken to prepare the civil population for a war emergency. Such arrangements as they had made for defence were inhibited by the credulity and hesitancy of the government. Churchill remarked to the House of Commons on 11 April,

> It is not the slightest use blaming the allies for not being able to give substantial help and protection to neutral countries if we are held at arm's length until these neutrals are actually attacked on a scientifically prepared plan by Germany...

# CHAPTER TEN

## 'THE WAY OF THE GODS'

As Hitler acquired power among the German people and sought to extend his sovereignty through Europe towards domination of the world, the government of Japan pursued expansion throughout the Far East with the aim of creating 'a world under one roof'. The coincidence in aim and time of these manifestations, the common use of political terrorism and military force, the correspondence in philosophy of a pure and chosen people extending their rule over inferior races suggests a close similarity between the aggression of Germany and Japan – even a partnership.

Coincidence in time and aim there certainly was, and a random partnership, as much neglected as used.★ Some other common-alities persisted, despite markedly dissimilar development as international powers.

Germany's course ran through the defeat of Prussian liberalism by Bismarck in association with the army, his use of the army to assist in the gathering of the German states under the Prussian king rather than the Austrian emperor, and his assertion of authority over the army when it had served its purpose politically. The upshot was the concentration of power in the hands of the king as emperor of Germany in 1870, a power subsequently used by the sovereign *inter alia* to rid himself of Bismarck. The attempt of Austria to expand thereafter into the Balkans led unwittingly to the gigantic and prolonged clash of arms into which almost all the European nations, the British Empire, Japan and eventually the United States were drawn. The top-heavy monarchies of Germany,

---

★   In the Anti-Comintern Pact of 1936, Germany, Italy and Japan undertook not to enter a treaty with Russia except by mutual agreement. Hitler ignored this in 1939. He did not inform Japan about the invasion of Russia. The Japanese concluded a neutrality pact with Russia in 1941 without consulting Germany and withheld their plans for war except for a last-minute warning.

Austria-Hungary and Russia, and the eagerness of France to recover its lost provinces, had diminished the stability of Europe. The military victory of 1918 did not restore it. Hence, as observed earlier, the success of Hitler's opportunism.

Whilst Japan's development as an international aggressor was doubtless encouraged and accelerated by European instability and its concomitant, American isolationism, it took place over a greater period and was characterised by very different circumstances.

Japan emerged from a closed mediaeval society in 1865 with the overthrow of the Tokugawa shoguns and restoration of power to the Meiji emperor, then fourteen years old. The prime cause of change was a collapsing economy and the impetus of an American naval expedition under Commodore Matthew C. Perry in 1853, demanding open trade on behalf of his government. Restraints on foreign commerce were lifted by the new administration and, in what seemed to be a sign of political modernisation, a constitution was drafted which included the formation of a legislature. Yet politically and socially much remained essentially unchanged.

Those who directly or by their support restored imperial rule had no intention of shaping a constitutional monarchy. They did not comprehend such a system. It was foreign to their experience and nature. The aim was to preserve the order of life in Japan while adapting to the requirements of a modern trading power. That order was based on a system of strong central authority with descending tiers embracing the elders of each family. At all levels, respect and obedience was to be accorded to superiors. Those who sought to change the established order, for example, in seeking power for themselves, had been suppressed by the professional soldiers of the shogunate, the *samurai*.* Clans subordinate to the Tokugawa had been permitted to retain, within limits, their own *samurai*, who united when the nation was attacked by foreigners.

The men who became the emperor's ministers – with one exception of *samurai* descent – decided that this system no longer suited the requirement for internal security, and was inadequate for defence against external attack. The intrusion of Commodore Perry and his American warships had demonstrated the latter point beyond question. Conscription was introduced. The fittest young

---

* This body numbered about two million in a populace of thirty million. It was too powerful to be paid off in quiet times.

men in character and physique would be trained for two – later three – years in a modernised army and navy. A strong reserve would be built up as each class returned to civil life.

These considerations were part of a wider review of policy. The opening of the empire to trade with commercial powers such as the Americans, British, Dutch and Russians provided short-term benefits to Japan's economy but the concessions made in the process soon became obnoxious. Tariffs were decided by foreign governments. Japanese courts were not permitted to decide matters of commercial law; were denied even the right to try foreigners residing in Japan who broke its laws. Lacking political experience and commercial weight – the potential for exports was limited – the Japanese hierarchy had none the less expected that their nation-state, which they believed to be superior to all others, would rapidly take its place among the great powers in the world beyond their shores. Instead, the inherent weaknesses of their ignorance, economic structure and resources were rapidly exposed. It was not, of course, seen like this by those in power in Japan. They were already engaged in modulating the form of imperial government for the better administration of the nation and the conduct of external relations. Externally, it seemed, the essential requirement of a power was military clout. Japan needed strong, modern armed forces to attain equal status with those who sought to impose such terms and conditions; and to seize territory elsewhere to expand the national economic base. These ideas were consonant with the pride and energy of the Japanese people.

To consolidate power, the ruling oligarchy drafted a constitution in these terms:

> The empire of Japan shall be reigned over and governed by a line of emperors unbroken for ages eternal ... The emperor is sacred and inviolable ... combining in himself the rights of sovereignty, and exercises them according to the provisions of the present constitution.

Upon the existing influences of Buddhism and Confucianism, there was to be laid a third, *kami no michi*, 'the way of the gods', a reanimation by the state of a religion rooted in the sun-goddess and all nature. It is known popularly by the Chinese word, *Shinto*. The emperor, traditionally a descendant of the sun-goddess, was worshipped as a divine being. His remoteness had enabled the shoguns to usurp temporal power. The oligarchy, monopolising access to the emperor, now similarly ruled in his name. The restoration of the emperor's authority had not, however, been accomplished by men solely concerned with acquiring personal political power. To one extent or another all believed that the shogunate was improper, perhaps sacrilegious. It was not a matter of expediency but of duty to make imperial sovereignty absolute. A programme was launched to remind the nation that the emperor was heaven-sent, sacred, virtuous, all-wise – educating all classes and conditions of the people to venerate, love, honour and obey him. This inevitably excluded any discussions of his right to rule.

# CHAPTER ELEVEN

# THE WAY OF THE WARRIOR

The new Japanese constitution was finally promulgated in 1889. The election of a legislature and subsequent formation of political parties suggested to the Western powers that they were watching the evolution of parliamentary democracy in Japan. It was as inconceivable to those governed by such a system in Europe and America that the description of the emperor's powers was to be taken literally as it was to the oligarchy in Japan that it should be applied in any other way.

Nevertheless, political factions emerged. Broadly, there was dissension among those who had access to power on two issues: the extent of military expenditure, and the extent and pace of modernisation. Over the years into the twentieth century there were many shades of view on these issues and matters of domestic policy. But there was no disagreement that progress towards recognition as an international power would be dependent on military strength. It was not a matter of self-defence – Japanese territory was not threatened – but of offence; expansion by military action. The *samurai* who had become politicians, those who had become leaders of the national armed forces, the old nobility with whom the *samurai* merged as a class into a new aristocracy, and the most powerful of the bankers, manufacturers and merchants whose fiefs would gradually fall to new leaders from *samurai* families – all were as much in agreement on that as on the status of the emperor.

Two nations were selected early as prey: China and Korea. The great empire of China was decaying fast in the second half of the nineteenth century. Korea was a small kingdom within China's sphere of influence and protection. The terrorisation of the latter led predictably to conflict with the former. In 1894–5, a handful of Japanese divisions defeated a Chinese host. But the latter were crudely commanded and poorly armed – and their supply arrangements were chaotic. The Japanese fielded a modest but balanced force of all arms, well led, controlled by a trained staff and comprehensively equipped. Their supply lines were assured by a small modern navy trained and organised by the British. The Liaotung peninsula in north-east China, Wei-hai-wei in Shantung, Taiwan and the Pescadores were taken as spoils of war with an indemnity of 200 million *tael* of silver, which funded Japanese war expenditure comfortably.

Then France, Germany and Russia intervened to insist on the return of Chinese mainland territory. The Japanese nation was outraged; when the government complied it was obliged to resign. Its successor decided to increase the strength of the army from seven to twelve divisions, the navy fivefold. The term of conscription was extended from two to three years, with nine years on the reserve. A national armaments industry was created to include capacity for the manufacture of capital warships and the largest possible guns. By this means Japanese power would be raised to a level which would make it possible to defy the *diktat* of the Europeans.

As it happened, the United States and most European powers were impressed by the Japanese victory in China. The relinquishment of extra-territorial rights on Japanese territory and a settlement on tariffs were nudged towards completion as a consequence. Another outcome was the acceptance that Korea now lay within the sphere of Japanese influence, an understanding that irked the faction in the Russian government seeking to expand in the Orient. Port Arthur on the Liaotung peninsula was being developed from 1898 as a Russian naval base.* Encouraged by the tsar, a Siberian timber company began cutting arbitrarily inside Korea. Russian troops, brought in as part of an international force to suppress the Boxers,† continued to occupy the greater part of

---

\* Having forced Japan to abandon its conquest of the Liaotung peninsula, including Port Arthur, Russia took it from China in 1898 as the result of an international foray to avenge the murder of two German missionaries. Germany siezed concessions in Shantung at this time, Britain took Wei-hai-wei.

† The Boxers, members of a Chinese peasant movement, the Society of the Right and Harmonious Fists, were originally opposed to the ruling Ch'ing (Manchu) dynasty but began attacking foreigners in 1899. With the approval of the aged empress, the international legations in Peking were besieged in 1900 until they were relieved by an international force. At this time Russian troops occupied the whole of north-east China.

north-east China despite assurances that these would be withdrawn. In retaliation, on 9 February 1904, without any formal declaration of war, a Japanese destroyer force entered Port Arthur in darkness to bombard the Russian fleet at anchor. Two armies were launched to challenge the Russian land forces, one of which became locked in a colossal struggle for the Chinese provincial capital, Mukden.

Japanese soldiers displayed over the following months a bravery described by the Russians as 'fanatical'. The outcome of the war was decided at sea, however. The Russians sailed their Baltic fleet halfway round the world as a reinforcement. It was annihilated by Admiral Togo's warships as it attempted to pass through the Tsushima Strait in May 1905. Other powers, in particular Britain, were not displeased. The Japanese had obligingly discouraged Russian expansion east of Suez. This seemed to underline the value of the Anglo-Japanese Alliance concluded in 1902. The British government made no objection when Japan annexed Korea in 1910.

The notion of Japan as an aggressive power now began to take root in the United States. Others, notably Germany, were more apprehensive of China's potential for growth. What caught international attention generally was the manufacturing capacity in Japan for capital and consumer goods, an observation soon counterbalanced by the reflection that Japanese talent was limited to copying the skills of Western industry. Innovation apparently eluded them.

Perhaps the most important consequence of the war against Russia for the Japanese people was the raising of their self-confidence. They had taken on a European power, superior in numbers, ostensibly more advanced in the technique and technology of modern warfare, and beaten it. This glorious outcome had an effect quite unexpected by those devoted to the *samurai* tradition. Political philosophies of the outside world which had percolated among educated people in Japanese society – and subsequently among skilled workers in the rapidly growing urban areas – began to interact with the virtues of personal restraint and social harmony prescribed by Confucianism and Buddhism. Factions in the *Diet* (legislature) reflecting this development became critical of aggressive expansion as a policy and contested the growth of defence spending in the budget and the influence of generals and admirals as government ministers.

Japan's entry in the First World War as an ally of Britain and France led to a closing of national ranks. Its trade boomed in war and other manufactures. The German possessions in China and the northern Pacific fell to Japan. The triumph of the democracies in 1918 stirred again the idea that this alien system might be desirable. The victory of the Russian revolution also inspired a scattering of Japanese workers and intellectuals. The return to China of the Shantung concessions at Versailles did not vex the whole Japanese nation; and there was no general sense of defeat when the anti-Bolshevik expedition in Siberia failed in 1921. The army and navy began to fear that pacifism and political pluralism were taking root in Japan.

In seeking to reverse this process, the two armed services, particularly the army, were hindered by loss of public esteem and internal struggles.

The first of these was due more to a failing economy than to the persistent arrogance of the military. From being a creditor nation during the First World War, Japan rapidly became a debtor. There were rice riots shortly after the armistice. Industry began to lay off labour. Partly due to governmental incompetence, the post-war boom elsewhere was of little help to Japan and the effect of the 1929 collapse was severe. For a little while, the wartime prestige of the forces was maintained. A British officer attached to a regiment in Honshu reported in 1919, 'At every place at which we halted we were given tea and, generally, fruit and cakes as well by the local inhabitants...' By 1921 soldiers, particularly non-commissioned officers alone or in small groups, were beaten up by labourers on numerous occasions. If the handle of an officer's sword touched a fellow passenger on public transport his spurs were kicked off. Cakes were not then offered to marching troops; indeed, they were often refused water by the country people. In the towns and cities, Socialism was manifest, the newly formed Communist Party active. Soldiers were seen breaking strikes or putting down worker's demonstrations, sometimes with bullet and bayonet. A popular theme in the *Diet* and press was that the army and navy were spending a high proportion of the falling national income. In the countryside, resentment was chiefly due to the long term of conscription which kept young men from work on farms and family plots of land.

Just before noon on 1 September 1923, a natural disaster

transformed these circumstances. A huge earthquake shook Tokyo, the capital, and the surrounding area, including the port and city of Yokohama. The police and fire services were overwhelmed. The army and navy came rapidly and effectively to the rescue. Three months of this work, reported in all newspapers, earned the praise of the nation. But it did not stay the movement for reduction of the armed forces among politicians.

The army's ability to react positively to this demand was inhibited by internal dissensions. These were scarcely apparent to outsiders, though there were some indications of a division between ultra-Conservatives, who saw no reason to modernise the army's technology, and those who protested that the weapons and tactics of the Russo-Japanese war would not bring any victories in the 1920s or 30s. But there were personal divisions and dissatisfactions among the officers which were spoken of only between close friends – chiefly the resentment of those who were not of or descended from the Choshu and Satsuma *samurai*, whose members had been principals in the overthrow of the Tokugawa clan. The most powerful of these was Yamagata Arimoto who had become a field marshal and prince and, though an octogenarian in 1920, was still pulling strings to ensure that Choshu men were receiving promotion and appointments in the Cabinet as well as in the armed forces. All military and most matters of foreign policy of any importance were put to him until his death in 1922.

Secret societies were formed to break the Choshu faction. Others were concerned to improve the poor pay and conditions of the regular element of the army and navy, the cadre of officers, warrant and non-commissioned officers, who commanded and trained the conscripts before returning them to the reserve as officers or other ranks. A pre-war saying, '*Bimbo shoi, yattoko chui, yarikuri taii*' ('Second lieutenants penniless, first lieutenants struggling, captains barely surviving') was now more than ever applicable. There was also a movement which deplored the soft living of the urban middle and upper classes. The ideas of many groups overlapped, especially in the need for modernisation of their service. All held in common with their superiors the need for a return of the nation to the principles of *bushido*, the way of the warrior.

Struggles for power in policy-making among the senior officers – struggles inevitably at that time between fellow Choshu officers – began to fall away with the final ascendancy of General Tanaka

Giichi as minister for war and his protégé and successor, General Ugaki Kazushige.* The reduction in naval expenditure brought about by the Washington Naval Conference in 1921[†] permitted political concentration on a reduction in army expenditure. Ugaki determined that there should be reductions in manpower – the conscription term would be reduced from three to two years – and also in the size of the standing army by adoption of the 'triangular' system – three companies in each of three battalions in each of three regiments in a division. At the same time, he appropriated part of the savings thus made to modernise weapons and equipment. The artillery was developed from old-fashioned direct to indirect fire; tanks and aircraft were introduced. Medium machine-guns and modern mortars were disposed to infantry battalions; and in the rifle companies of these units the light machine-gun became the prime weapon of the section or squad.

Ugaki was concerned no less to consolidate army popularity and authority after the earthquake. Public memories were short, opinions fickle. Reduction of the military budget would be well received but would earn only short-term dividends; soon he would be expected to offer more economies. The numbers and influence of liberals were growing among the educated classes. Socialism seemed to have taken root in the industrial workshops. Both were at variance with the thesis that the nation must be strong militarily if it was to grow as a political and commercial power in the world. The officer corps believed, too, that the new and alien philosophies threatened the moral health of the nation because they involved goals of personal prosperity and soft living. Moral and physical fitness would be assured only by the virtues of *bushido*: frugality, hard work, loyalty, obedience, self-discipline and manifest selflessness in the service of the emperor. Apprehending that much of society in the cities and major towns was growing indifferent, inimical even, to these ideas, Ugaki decided that the army should build its strength in those centres where the old values prevailed, among the country towns, villages and hamlets.

---

* Ugaki was not a Choshu officer.
† The conference was called as part of the movement for post-war disarmament. It prescribed the maintenance of capital warships in the ratio 5:5:3 for the United States, United Kingdom and Japan. Although this raised the latter to the position of third naval power in the world, the Japanese believed that they had been tricked into accepting a constraint.

Two organisations offered a base for this project: the Imperial Military Reserve Association, founded in 1910, and the Greater Japan Youth Association, both conceived by General Tanaka as a means of enhancing the quality and readiness of military power. General Ugaki had assisted in the formation of the latter. He was also well aware that men in the reserve, brought up in the old order, were influential in their villages as organisers and members of the fire brigade, the road-mending forces – foremost in good works. In many places they also ran local home guard units, drilling and otherwise training volunteers in case of war, but more immediately in watch and ward against criminals. The Youth Association aimed to educate young men in patriotism and in physical culture to prepare them for the services – physical and moral fitness were looked for when the examiners made their annual tour to pick out young men for military duty. Some of the enthusiasm had passed out of these organisations in the difficult post-war resettlement.

With a surplus of regular officers, General Ugaki passed many to the Ministry of Education, making an initial subvention from army funds towards their salaries. They would work among the rustic youth, revitalising *bushido*, moulding 'national villagers'.

In 1926, the range of their work was extended. Youth work, which included military drill, was undertaken in the middle schools. A small number of the students then graduated to upper or high schools while the remainder went to work. Either way, contact was lost with all these teenage boys during working hours until they were selected for conscription for regular service at the age of twenty or passed to the reserve training scheme.* General Ugaki decided that he would form, through the Ministry of Education, youth training centres for those who went to work. These boys, aged between fifteen and twenty, would be given 800 hours of part-time education annually: 400 hours of drill, 100 hours in 'ethics'

---

* The army and navy did not take all young men fit for active service annually at the age of twenty; there were too many for the number of ships, army units and rear organisations maintained in peace. Those fit, but not called, passed immediately into the first reserve in which they were given basic training locally. With those who were in regular service, they formed the First National Army, remaining available for training and mobilisation until they were forty. Others, fit for limited service, were placed, without training, in the Second National Army. Very few young men in the countryside had no military training at all due to the military education system in middle school years and the youth training centres.

and the remainder in the Japanese language, arithmetic and various kinds of technical training. The scheme did not extend immediately among the whole range of technical and supplementary schools, but embraced deliberately the country population. By the 1930s the success of the scheme and changes in political perceptions permitted absorption of all part-time educational establishments for young people, including girls. The latter were encouraged on graduating to join the National Defence Women's Association.

By this means, slowly but surely, between 1925 and 1931, the army began to inculcate its spirit and philosophy among the majority of the Japanese people. Within country towns, the villages and hamlets, the programme was enhanced by the activities of the reserve association who were leaders and exemplars in almost every local service. In conjunction with community elders they created an expectation of good behaviour among boys and young men. Early rising, drill, mock bayonet exercise or other physical pursuits followed by a day's work militated against late hours. Heavy drinking in taverns was considered a disgrace to the community. Harmonious behaviour was expected. The army became yet more popular with farmers, large and small, when the period of regular service was cut from three to two years due to budget pressures in 1927.

During those years, Japan's foreign policy was generally conciliatory. Differences were settled with the Russian Communist government following its consolidation of authority throughout the old empire. Chiang Kai-shek's National government of China was recognised in January 1929. Within the army, however, the conviction had strengthened that national interests were being disregarded abroad while soft living and socialism were corrupting morals at home. The apparent drift of government towards democratic practice was regarded as the reason for a failing economy. The population had risen to seventy million. Rice production was stationary and indequate to feed this number. Imported rice was expensive and so, too, were the raw materials Japan needed for its industrial complex. Overseas markets for manufactured products were difficult to find. Silk prices fell by 50 per cent. It did not matter that other powers were similarly distressed in 1929 and for several years following by the financial crisis. Officers considered that their country should look to its own interests by returning to a policy of expansion.

In September 1931, beginning as an initiative of the local commander but backed soon by the high command at home, Japanese forces in north-east China and Korea used a minor clash with the troops of the local warlord,* the notorious 'Manchurian incident', to occupy the entire territory. Chiang Kai-shek appealed to the League of Nations; he had barely sufficient forces to maintain authority in a huge land given to warlordism and insurgent Communism, none to eject the Japanese. Within China he instituted a boycott of Japanese goods. Incidents between Chinese and Japanese soldiers on the boundary of the international settlement in Shanghai developed into a local war. Forty-three thousand Japanese soldiers were concentrated in the area, pushing out the defenders. Meanwhile, the province of north-east China was declared to be an independent state, Manchu-kuo. A member of the Manchu family was placed on an emperor's throne by Japanese power.† Proposals by the League, following a commission of enquiry, that the territory should be returned to China with some recognition of Japanese interests, were rejected in Tokyo. Japan withdrew from membership of the League and within a year had extended its occupation of China southwards to the Great Wall, spilling over it. Chiang was obliged to accept a demilitarised zone south of the Wall with Japan in control to the north.

These were the activities of the army abroad, initiating operations independently of government. Attempts to reduce the armed forces by budgetary measures resulted in the assassination of a minister in November 1930 and that of a former finance minister and the head of the Mitsui corporation in February 1932. In May of that year, young naval and army officers murdered the prime minister, attacked police headquarters, banks and several political party headquarters in Tokyo. At their trial, the group explained that they were seeking to save the nation by smashing democratic practice, the *Diet*, bureaucracy, and economic reliance on Western-style business and industry. Many were ready to declare them

---

\* North-east China had been the fief of the powerful Marshal Chang Tso-lin. He had been succeeded by his son, 'the Young Marshal', Chang Hsueh-liang, who was unwilling to maintain good relations with the Japanese garrison.

† Dedicated themselves to imperial service, the Japanese government believed that the enthronement of the Manchu heir, Pu Yi, would reconcile the Chinese people to the loss of a huge region of their country. There was no more support for the restoration of the Manchu than there had been for the Ming dynasty. It was a gross misjudgement, a late example of Japan's political naïvety.

young heroes. Even the public prosecutor accepted that their motive was admirably patriotic. The influence of moderate politicians began to wane. Some were later to confess that they were so terrorised by these and lesser incidents that they withdrew from public life.

It was not only the conservatives in the countryside who applauded the ideals of the assassins. Many city dwellers had become disenchanted with Western influence. Hard times had contributed to this but so had the withdrawal of friendship by Britain and the United States. The former had not renewed the Anglo-Japanese Treaty, due principally to the wishes of the United States, and, in 1924, the American government had passed an act which permanently denied Japanese immigration. A national humiliation day in Tokyo gathered huge crowds. The theme of speeches was 'hate America'. The suspicion that Japan had been duped into naval disarmament at the Washington conference was revived; the myth became accepted as a fact. The political assumption that disarmament generally would be possible because of a developing friendship with the United States was denounced.

———

Japan's formal withdrawal from the League of Nations took effect in March 1935. Her representatives withdrew also from the international naval conference of 1936 when denied an upper limit of arms in common with the United States and United Kingdom. At home, the army minister was propagating the notion that a crisis was developing due to threats from several directions: from China, resentful of the Manchurian settlement; from Russia, seen to be increasing its Far Eastern force; and from the United States, reportedly engaged in rebuilding its fleets. He might have added a fourth: from within the homeland. Two Cabinet ministers and the inspector-general of military training were murdered on 26 February 1936, and attempts made on the lives of the prime minister and three other senior officers and statesmen. The assassins were twenty-one officers, three cadet surgeons and ten civilians, supported by 1,500 troops who simply obeyed their superiors. The principals expressed similar aims to those tried in 1932. The army ranks were purged of sympathisers solely, it was declared, as a matter of discipline; internally, the high command made it clear that it had not lost its resolve to lead the nation back to a purer and more honourable course. The regular and reserve forces were reminded that the army was being modernised and strengthened.* In November 1936 the Anti–Comintern Pact was signed with Germany and a description of its aims and advantages was circulated among all ranks.

The invasion of China was begun in July 1937, once more as the result of an 'incident', on this occasion close to Peking. Without authorisation from the government, the commander-in-chief in Manchuria launched a force down the north China railway. Landings were made in Hangchow Bay. Nanking, the Chinese capital, was taken in December. By October 1938, Hankow and Canton had fallen. Although the warlords had made common cause with Chiang Kai-shek, the direction of operations, standards of individual and collective proficiency and the services of supply in the Nationalist Army remained inferior. Despite its huge population, China could not effectively counter-attack.

At the end of 1938, the Japanese government offered peace on the following terms:

Chinese recognition of the state of Manchu-kuo
Chinese adherence to the Anti-Comintern Pact
Chinese consent to the presence of Japanese troops in specified
    areas of China and Inner Mongolia
Freedom of residence, trade and development of resources by
    Japan in China and Inner Mongolia

Given agreement to these points, Japan would withdraw its forces and make no claim for indemnity.

These conditions, unacceptable to the Chinese government as they certainly were to the Chinese people, were also offensive to the United States. But the offence was taken primarily because Japanese aircraft had sunk an American gunboat on the Yangtse river and strafed those trying to escape ashore. There was also sympathy for the refugees shown on the newsreels at the movies and reported by the press. Although the US Navy persuaded its

---

* Further retrenchment of armaments had been accepted for 1932 but the 'Manchurian incident' of that year caused its abandonment. A temporary 'army replenishment' was accepted to meet the commitment. This was due to end in 1935. By that financial year, agreement was given to comprehensive rearmament to modernise the technology of the army and to increase the numbers called up annually to bring capability to that of a first-class power by 1940.

secretary to tell the president in Cabinet that it wanted to go to war over its lost gunboat, the president replied, 'Claude [Swanson], I am a pacifist.' His Cabinet knew he was not but they believed with him that events in China were not threatening America directly any more than events in Germany were at this time. However regrettable, they were the affair of others.

This opinion was not wholly wrong at that moment. As the war continued in China, a dogged resistance by the defenders and the expanse of their land combined to deny a complete victory to Japan. There was discouragement also in a bloody and unsuccessful struggle between Japanese and Russian forces on the borders of Outer Mongolia. Hitler's pact with Russia, made secretly but necessarily revealed in the defeat of the Poles, mocked the Anti-Comintern agreement. The administration in Tokyo fell as a consequence. Two short-lived governments followed under moderate men from the army and navy. But as Hitler succeeded with one victory after another to the summer of 1940, the army forced a change on the basis that plums were to be had in east Asia for the picking: French Indo-China, Malaya and the Dutch East Indies. These were fruits that would transform Japan's economy and political power. They would permit the creation of what was seen as the 'Greater East Asia Co-Prosperity Sphere'.

Yet there were still some statesmen capable of political restraint in Japan. The new elders who advised the emperor were former prime ministers. They brought Prince Konoye into office, a confidant of the emperor. He was not willing to launch an attack on Malaya and the Dutch East Indies but agreed that they should press Vichy France to grant air bases in northern Indo-China, and the United Kingdom to close the Burma Road, China's back-door supply route. Somewhat to the surprise of the army, both requests were agreed to in August by governments anxious to avoid fresh difficulties.* In September 1940, Japan made a tripartite pact binding itself to enter the war in alliance with Germany and Italy if the United States should join with Britain. As a counterweight, incidentally paying Hitler back in his own coin, a neutrality pact was made with Russia in the following April and, after much discussion, talks between Tokyo and Washington were proposed to settle differences. The army minister, General Tojo Hideki,

* Britain reopened the Burma Road on 18 October 1940.

supported the prime minister when the foreign minister, Matsuoka, objected to this last initiative. But it was Matsuoka who conducted the negotiations. Unknown to him, the Americans had broken the Japanese diplomatic code. Seeing the instructions sent to the Japanese ambassador in June 1941, President Roosevelt noted, 'they seem to me to be the product of a mind which is deeply disturbed and unable to think quietly or logically.'

There was now little doubt in Washington that America was on the edge of war. All that was needed to destroy the remnants of isolationism was a *casus belli*. But Roosevelt's inclination to help Britain had now to be tempered by the manifest upsurge of Japanese activities in the Pacific and the indications of the broken diplomatic codes. The president had been advised that the army and navy needed time to prepare the Philippines and uprate the fleets. He was ready to keep talking with Japan therefore while there was any chance of a settlement, but it seemed increasingly misguided to continue to supply American strategic goods to the war reserves of a potential enemy. When the Japanese government demanded sea, land and air bases in southern Indo-China from the French in July 1941, President Roosevelt put an embargo on all strategic materials for Japan. Britain and the Netherlands followed suit. At once the naval high command in Tokyo, which had stood back from those who counselled war, joined their ranks. Despite extraordinary purchases, however, their oil reserves stood at only four months' usage. They had relied on eighteen before the outbreak of any war.* Prince Konoye's government fell. His place was taken by General Tojo Hideki.

---

\* Due in part to operational demands in China, Japanese oil stocks fell from a peak of fifty-one million barrels in 1939 to about forty million by the middle of 1941. Approximately 90 per cent of Japan's oil came from the United States and the Dutch East Indies.

# CHAPTER TWELVE

# PEACETIME ATTITUDES, WARTIME SITUATIONS

In later years it has been suggested that, with the appointment of General Tojo as prime minister, Japan was irrevocably committed to war. Whilst it is true that he had long abandoned support for the Konoye policy of persuasive diplomacy, he let negotiations for a peaceful settlement run on, though every day was shortening the capacity for options. He had a remit from a conference of 6 September 1941 to limit the duration of talks with the Americans to the month of November. Beyond December, oil stocks would fall short of the requirements for a full-scale attack on the targets to the south. Whatever the term of these operations, another period had to be added for the transportation to Japan of oil and other strategic necessities such as bauxite, rubber and tin.

Over the preceding year there had been almost continuous discussion concerning strategy in the Army and Naval General Staffs, in government and in the Liaison Conference – a policy-making body attended periodically by the emperor which brought together politicians including the elder statesmen and senior service officers. When Hitler attacked Russia, Matsuoka among others – 'the northwarders' – advocated participation to seize Russian territory but, other considerations apart, the potential gains were not worth the risks. In China, most major cities and ports had fallen to the Japanese forces but they controlled scarcely a third of the mainland. The Dutch East Indies, producing sixty-five million barrels of oil a year, were the most attractive of the southern territories. Malaya was also rich in many things Japan needed. Attacking the Dutch East Indies would almost certainly bring about war with Britain, which had a major base in Singapore, and perhaps with the United States. To ensure safe passage of oil and dry cargoes back to the home islands it would be necessary to 'neutralise' both Singapore and the Philippines. An attack on the latter would surely involve America.

The hierarchy of the army and navy, whose ideas were based principally on staff studies until the summer of 1941, believed that they could 'complete these operations in the southern territory in six months'. The emperor reminded the army that it had failed to reduce China in four years. Even so, war seemed the only option unless the United States could be persuaded to lift its trading ban and resume normal commerce. The United States would only do that if Japan withdrew from Indo-China and China.

While the discussions continued, the Army and Naval General Staffs and certain of the commanders-in-chief of operational forces advanced their concepts and plans for war, accelerating this process from July 1941 when the trade embargo took effect. The head of the army operations directorate in Tokyo believed that 'no one can doubt any longer that we are being forced into war to preserve our people'. This was a reiteration of the view that a nation too populous for its land mass had the right to seize the territory and wealth of others by force of arms. The services, overwhelmingly the army, had brought Japan to its dilemma. Ironically, with a major war in Europe, the opportunities for trade in which Japan excelled were rising fast but, by the autumn of 1941, any attempt to remain neutral, and thereby reverse the ideas fostered of a nation dedicated to the *bushido* philosophy, would have been unacceptable to a considerable element of the Japanese nation. At his trial after the war, General Tojo commented that he had retained the portfolios of the War and, additionally, the Home Ministry, on becoming prime minister because 'he faced a fearful trend foreboding internal confusion if peace was decided upon instead of war'. This was not the strategem, once observed by Dr Johnson, of a scoundrel seeking a last refuge in patriotism. He was stating a fact. Among the people, the education programme over which he, among others, had presided had been only too successful, expanding from the countryside to influence many in the cities, despite residual cores of liberal, Socialist and Communist conviction. Within the officers corps, secret societies dedicated to expansion by war had coalesced and attracted new members. Bitterness and envy concerning the preferential promotion and appointment of those from the Choshu and Satsuma families, a practice which was in any case declining, was no longer seriously divisive. All were enthused by the thought that Japan would imminently assert its power throughout Asia. The German conquests were much admired, taken as proof that the great commercial powers were vulnerable to attack, though some officers were far from sure that Britain was already defeated. The way of the Japanese was surely, no less than that of the Germans, the way of the warrior.

While General Tojo left open the decision for peace or war, influenced perhaps by the evident opposition of the emperor to the latter, the armed forces brought their plans and arrangements to completion. Troops were embarked and sailed to reinforce southern Indo-China. Other troop transports and store ships were gathering for loading, their escorts to hand. Still, on 25 November, the option of war had not finally been chosen. Japan's proposals were being considered in Washington: evacuation of its forces from southern Indo-China; a settlement of Pacific issues leading to a withdrawal from Indo-China altogether; an opportunity to nego-tiate with China free from United States interference. In return the United States would at once resume supply of oil to Japan and normal trade, and assist her to secure the products of the East Indies. Both powers would agree not to advance by arms into the southern Pacific or north-east Asia.

On 26 November 1941, Cordell Hull, US secretary of state, responded with ten points which included demands that Japan should at once withdraw all its forces, including police, from Indo-China and China, and recognise the Nationalist government as sovereign in the latter. It was the end of bargaining. On the 29th, war was chosen unreservedly in Tokyo. There was no sudden launching of forces; submarines, surface ships and troops were already moving to implement war plans. They would now proceed to these unchecked. There would be no prior declaration of hostilities.* Operations were to begin by surprise, but not quite to the extent of Hitler's practice of surprising even his closest allies. The following instruction was sent to the Japanese ambassador in Berlin:

---

\* To avoid a charge of bad faith by the United States, it was arranged that a lengthy document, concluding with a declaration of war, would be handed to the US secretary of state by the Japanese ambassador in Washington at the hour of attack. Due to mishandling in the embassy, it was delivered an hour late.

Say very secretly to them [the German government] that there is an extreme danger that war may suddenly break out between the Anglo-Saxon nations and Japan through some clash of arms, and add that the time of the breaking out of this war may come sooner than anyone dreams.

The overall strategy had been arrived at by considerations of four options, each of which had special merits relative to mounting arrangements.

The first option was the seizure of the oilfield territories – Borneo, Java and Sumatra – followed by attacks on Malaya and the Philippines. It gave primacy to seizure of the oilfields but was discarded because the British and Americans would be given time to recover from initial surprise. The second idea was to attack the Philippines, then the oil islands and finally Malaya. But Singapore was very close and the British might be able to launch a counter-offensive or reinforce the Dutch colonial forces. It was not adopted. The third option, a reverse of the second, left until last the Philippine island of Luzon, containing the main American naval and air bases and was discarded on that account. The fourth option was then chosen: a simultaneous offensive against the Philippines and Malaya followed by seizure of Borneo, Java, Sumatra and, with the British Far East base overcome, the oilfields of Burma. The Naval General Staff believed that the American Pacific Fleet was unlikely to sortie into Japanese waters. If it did, it would be worn down by light forces and then brought to battle by the Imperial Fleet.

That was the naval premise until August 1941. At the end of that month, Admiral Yamamoto, commander-in-chief of the combined sea and air fleet, revealed to the chief of naval staff, Admiral Nagano, another plan. They should attack the American fleet in its base at Pearl Harbor in the Hawaiian Islands at the outset of operations. Nagano responded that it would be extremely hazardous and was unnecessary. Pressed, he agreed to testing the idea in a war game. When this was run in September, the carrier-force commander, Vice-Admiral Nagumo, joined the opposition. He anticipated that he would lose at least two of the six aircraft carriers, all of which would be needed to cover the southern operations.

Yamamoto would not give way. He argued that to leave the United States Pacific Fleet unscathed, able to mobilise and make ready for action as Japan commenced the huge maritime operation in the south, was to invite defeat. At the very least an American sea and air attack against them during its course would delay progress. Japanese forces would run out of the time needed to bring the resources from the Malay archipelago into use. It was a strong argument but insufficient to win Nagano over. Yamamoto had to threaten to resign before his plan was accepted on 3 November.

The Pearl Harbor project effectively settled the date of opening the war: X-Day; moon and weather jointly suggested a final approach to the Hawaiian Islands on Sunday 8 December.* The timetable, based on Tokyo clocks, ran as follows:

0215 – landings at Kota Bharu in Malaya
0325 – attack on Pearl Harbor
0400 – landings on the Kra Isthmus, Thailand
0530 – (assuming success at Pearl Harbor) aircraft launched from Taiwan against the Philippines prior to assault landings
0830 – (assuming lodgement in Malaya) Hong Kong to be invaded

Operations to capture Guam, Wake Island and the Gilberts were interspersed among these.

The dreadful story of Pearl Harbor fills volumes of print. A major defence establishment of a great and dynamic nation was taken completely by surprise, even though warning indicators were flashing in Washington and within the base itself. But the army commander thought the navy was patrolling the seas, which they were not; and the naval commander-in-chief thought the army was on full anti-aircraft alert, which they were not. The niceties of protocol and prerogative were consistently maintained. Fine budget disciplines militated. When shells were broken out of magazines on the American warships still in action after the first attack by Admiral Nagumo's aircraft, the fuses were locked into settings complying with peacetime safety rules. The one element of luck that ran with the Americans was the absence of their carrier force.

---

* The Hawaiian Islands being to the east of the international date line, the date of attack there was 7 December.

The whole system was oriented by the environment of peace: political, economic and social.

Thus the bell rang for the contest to begin in the Pacific. Its echoes met over the broad waters those from the bells ringing in Malaya and the Philippines.

# CHAPTER THIRTEEN

# THE CONQUEST OF MALAYA

If 8 December was the most suitable day for an attack upon Pearl Harbor, it was the last suitable day for landing the Japanese Twenty-Fifth Army in Malaya. By then the north-east monsoon would be developing. Sea and cloud conditions, in the view of the chief meteorologist on Formosa, would worsen thereafter, making beach operations hazardous until the following April. The General Staff – the army staff – thus wished to land as soon after midnight on the 7th as possible, using surprise. But the naval staff did not believe that surprise would be preserved: in all probability the convoys would be observed by patrolling British aircraft or submarines. There should be a full bombardment of the shore over some hours prior to the landing, with co-ordinated air strikes against Royal Air Force bases, even if this delayed the landings. When the joint commanders and staffs met in October to study the operation as a whole, hotheads among the army members were ready for high words. To their surprise, Vice-Admiral Ozawa, commanding the naval component, said at the outset, 'I know that there is a difference of view between us as to the type of landing to be made. I say that the navy should accept the army's proposals, even at the risk of annihilation.' It was a good augury for inter-service relationships in the undertaking.

The conference lacked the forceful presence of the army commander, Lieutenant-General Yamashita Tomoyuki, who was not appointed until 6 November. On balance, the news of his selection promoted confidence among the officers of the Twenty-Fifth Army, though there were superiors and subordinates who judged him to be a dangerous man, unstable and grossly ambitious.

A graduate of the War College, Yamashita had held a succession of important appointments in which he had earned a reputation for intelligence and practicality; but he had not been reluctant to tread on rivals among his peers during his service and had thus made enemies. In 1935, he had been appointed chief of military affairs, a key post in the Imperial general headquarters involving responsibility for mobilisation, national defence policy and the co-ordination of military expenditure. In the following year, at the time of the second junior officers' revolt, he became involved in mediation with those attempting to seize power because of his associations with secret military societies and factions. In the aftermath, he was forbidden entry to general headquarters and realised that his integrity was compromised. On the point of resignation, General (later Field-Marshal) Count Terauchi persuaded him to remain in the service. He was posted to the command of a division in Korea for eighteen months after which, to his surprise, he was promoted to lieutenant-general as inspector-general of the air force and hoped that this might lead to a return to one of the posts concerned with high policy matters. Instead, his next appointment was the command in north-east China. Umbrageous by nature, these events developed in Yamashita an acute sense of persecution. When he was informed that he was to command the operation in Malaya to capture Singapore, he ascribed the selection to the fact that there were many risks involved – mistakenly as it happened; he owed it to his reputation as a man who would press his force to the utmost. But he believed that General Tojo, the prime minister, would relish his difficulties. He had begun to mistrust his old protector, General Terauchi, under whose immediate command he was placed, and expected no loyalty from one of his subordinates, Lieutenant-General Nishimura Takuma.

Nishimura commanded the Imperial Guards Division, the tallest and most soldierly-looking men in the Japanese Army. They had not been in operations, however, since 1905. The bias of their training had been in ceremonial and the individual martial arts, with few opportunities for company- or higher-level exercises. Visiting the Guards on formation training, Yamashita told Nishimura that his division was manifestly unfit to take the field. Intensive training would be necessary prior to embarkation. The three other divisions in the Twenty-Fifth Army were the 5th, the 18th and the 56th, the former containing large numbers of officers and NCOs – regulars and recalled reservists – with battle experience in China. For reasons of his own – a gesture of defiant contempt for his superiors, perhaps – Yamashita dispensed with the

56th Division altogether and accepted the loss of an infantry regiment from the 18th Division, saying that he would conquer Malaya with the lesser number.*

The Twenty-Fifth Army headquarters was largely a collection of strangers; few of the staff officers had served together before, though inevitably some had been fellow cadets or students at the Staff College. They assembled in Saigon where they were joined early in November by the commander of 3rd Air Group, Lieutenant-General Sugawara, and his staff. Admiral Ozawa maintained an office in the same location to facilitate joint planning.

The capture of Malaya would provide Japan with many raw materials; but Singapore was the more attractive prize for the military. It contained the docks and repair facilities to service warships and merchantmen, the handling facilities and depots of a great port, communications and airfields. But more important of any of these, it was looked upon as the keep of the maritime gateway to Australasia and the Indian Ocean, and it was held by an occidental power.

Weather apart, four factors militated in the preparation of the operational plan: the ability to effect a secure lodgement in Malaya; the nature of the country; the circumstances of the enemy; and confidence in the quality of the Japanese Army, on land and in the air.

There was to be no hostile act of any kind in the Gulf of Thailand or against any other targets until the carrier-borne aircraft had been launched to strike Pearl Harbor. This influenced the form and area of the initial offensive. Political uncertainties as to the reactions of the Thai government and people to a Japanese incursion weighed against a principal thrust overland through central Thailand.[†] To minimise the chance of detection by British air or sea reconnais-

---

\* A Japanese Army headquarters commanded divisions directly – that is, there was no intermediate corps command echelon in between. The Guards and 5th Division were mechanised. The 18th Division had horse transport for its supply columns. Its 124th Regiment, half the infantry of the division, was detached for the operation to capture Borneo.

† Any attempt by the Japanese to invade Thailand from southern Indo-China before attacking Malaya would have alerted the defences of the latter. For their part, strongly influenced by the advice of the British ambassador in Bangkok, the British government would not permit the commander-in-chief, Far East, to launch forces pre-emptively into the Kra Isthmus until Thai neutrality was actually breached; a restraint that was lifted in the first week of December.

sance, the sea-borne assault force should be on passage for as short a time as possible. But there were insufficient assault landing-craft to put more than part of a division on the open beaches simultaneously in Malaya or on the neighbouring beaches of the Kra Isthmus.

The Japanese had recent information about the geography of southern Thailand and the Malay peninsula, the result of late reconnaissance. There were adequate beach approaches in the area, none of which was commanded by coastal guns. The governments of the Malay States and Straits Settlements* also published, in the interests of commerce and administration, details of areas under cultivation for rice, fruit, oil palm and rubber, conditions of roads, railways, bridges and tunnels, harbours and ports, minerals and mines, electric power and telephones. The various sources disclosed a largely mountainous country into which cultivation was extended from the low-lying coastal areas in north and central Malaya and from the southern portion, part of Pahang state and Johore. Many areas remained wild, either primary or, thicker yet, secondary jungle, where trees and underbrush had grown back on abandoned cultivation. The mouths of a dozen great rivers, fed by mountain streams, broke the sandy beaches on the east and west coasts. Elsewhere, the beaches gave way to mangrove swamps. At the foot of Malaya, connected by a causeway to the state of Johore, lay the sparkling city of Singapore.

In the peninsula proper, the majority people were the Malays; among them Indians, Tamils and Chinese who had arrived as labourers or traders over the years of development in the Straits Settlements. In Singapore, the Chinese predominated among this same mixture of peoples. The British governed the various territories and colonies and were ascendant in commerce, working hard and purposefully for the most part, but enjoying a life of domestic ease and relative affluence. By 1941, anxieties that the war might impinge upon these pleasant circumstances had receded. There had been troop and aircraft reinforcements and, latterly, an increase in naval strength. British, Australian and Indian forces were known to be stationed throughout Malaya. While no one

* The Straits Settlements comprised Singapore, Malacca, Penang and Province Wellesley; the Federated Malay States were Perak, Negri Sembilan, Pahang and Selangor; the unfederated states were Johore, Trengannu, Kedah and Perlis. The governor of the first two groups was high commissioner for the latter.

doubted that Japan might covet Malaya and Singapore, it was a common belief that they would not dare attack an area of such military strength.

The Japanese intelligence service, despite a late and daring piece of espionage by an officer from the headquarters of Twenty-Fifth Army, believed that the British field forces approximated to five divisions when the number was actually three.* They were not daunted by this. As recounted, General Yamashita dispensed with one of the divisions available to him. His subordinate commanders and staff believed that they and their soldiers were superior to the enemy. Though new to the environment, they had trained thoroughly in jungle warfare in south China and Indo-China. Their men were hardy, disciplined and ardent in battle. The standard of their leadership was high.

The fighting troops in the Twenty-Fifth Army were not well informed about the quality of the British and Imperial forces they would be fighting, but senior commanders and staff officers were familiar with the assessments made in Tokyo and from personal observations, principally in the Shanghai international settlement. The British were believed to be 'technically proficient', particularly the Royal Navy, but 'given to self-indulgence . . . demands on units are low'. The flying and fighting skills of the Royal Air Force were well regarded; the defeat of the *Luftwaffe* in the Battle of Britain had been reported from attachés in Europe and America, but it was known that many of the aircraft in squadron service in Malaya were old, no match for those flown by the Japanese. Speculative newspaper reports in the Straits and Hong Kong, giving high figures for reinforcements, were regarded as propaganda. Ideas about the Australians were mixed but concluded that they were sturdy men. There was a general expectation that the Indians, raised from subject peoples, might break quickly in battle. Some of these ideas, combined with a mass of practical information ranging from tactical tips to personal hygiene, and shot through with

---

* On 8 December, there were three Imperial divisions in Malaya, each with two brigades – 9th Indian, 11th Indian and 8th Australian – with a further two brigades and infantry outside these formations, totalling thirty battalions in all. These were supported by seven regiments (battalions) of 25-pounder guns, a mountain battery of light guns, and two anti-tank artillery regiments with 2-pounders. With anti-aircraft, engineer, signals and administrative units, these numbered 76,300 all ranks. There were no tanks in the force.

political indoctrination, were passed to every man in the army in a pamphlet entitled, 'Read This Alone and the War Can Be Won'.

In finalising the plan, the army high command was also determined to maximise the advantages of surprise and choice of offensive lines. The defenders must man their frontiers widely; the attacker would concentrate on a few chosen points. These were to be Singora and Patani in southernmost Thailand, and Kota Bharu on the north-east coast of Malaya. The 5th Division would land at the first two sites and push south with all speed to capture the airfield at Alor Star and the three main river crossings – including those of the Perak river – 200 miles to the south. A reinforced brigade of the 18th Division under Major-General Takumi would make the landing at Kota Bharu, closely followed by the remainder of that force. Once established, it would advance down the east coast to capture Kuantan, but be ready to switch to the western sector if there should be any hold-up there. The Guards would move through Thailand, catch up the 5th Division and be prepared to leap over that formation to assume the advance role. Progressively, the remainder of the army – tanks not committed with the leading divisions, heavy artillery and specialist engineers; and the third line of supply, transport, medical and repair services – would be landed through ports or across beaches or pass through Thailand. Twenty-Fifth Army headquarters would establish a tactical headquarters at Singora behind the first landings and be joined by its remaining elements later. The whole operation was to be covered by the 3rd Air Group with 459 aircraft, based initially in Indo-China until Thai and Royal Air Force airfields were brought into use. A further 159 naval aircraft were to assist during the landing phase.

These arrangements required considerable staff work and extensive briefing. Timings were fine. To ensure that everyone knew what to do in embarkation an exercise was held with as many ships as possible – some in use elsewhere did not arrive until a late hour – and there were similar loading trials for those making the overland journey.

The executive order was received by General Yamashita on 2 December 1941. 'It is predetermined that military operations begin on 8th December . . . ' He issued his own confirmatory orders on the 3rd, concluding with an exhortation to his subordinates. It 'became apparent to many of those present that this was indeed the eve of war . . . by which Japan would be able to shape its own destiny without being curbed by others.'* Emotions were stirred: some officers wept. One noted in his diary, 'a sense of dedication, a recognition of the opportunity for personal sacrifice'. Another experienced 'exaltation' as he left the conference.

Next day, the assault forces sailed from Hainan Island, the troops crammed aboard converted passenger and cargo ships, sleeping in shifts 'three to a mat', eating in shifts meals of rice or barley with bean paste and pickled radish. Some men had brought supplements; salt plums and dried eels were popular. Below the troop decks in selected vessels stood horses in temporary stalls. The animals were given a whiff of fresh air daily by the removal of hatches. Fortunately, it was not a long voyage.

═══════

As the aircraft aboard Admiral Nagumo's carriers made ready to launch against Pearl Harbor, the first wave of General Takumi's reinforced brigade was setting out from the anchored transports through a disturbed sea towards the Malayan shore – the first Japanese into action in the Second World War. Loading into the assault craft and other small boats had been difficult in the heavy swell. Those put into the first spent an uncomfortable hour waiting for the last to fill and make ready. At 01.00 General Takumi ordered the showing of a blue light, the signal that the first wave of boats should make for the shore.

The naval escort force was already firing but without significant effect; they did not know the precise sites of the beach defences. More immediately dangerous was the fact that the transports had been carried south in the coastal current. The assault craft were thus landing on beaches directly in front of the positions of the 3rd/17th Dogras, a battalion of the 8th Indian Infantry Brigade occupying reinforced concrete bunkers. At about 01.30, those watching from the sea saw a series of flashes and heard the sounds of artillery and small-arms fire along the beach.

The British high command in Singapore was aware that Japanese warships and transports were approaching on a course towards

---

* A caveat was made. If the United States should agree to the Japanese terms while the various forces were *en route* to their targets, they were to refrain from offensive action and withdraw. This was not well received during the briefings but in conversation afterwards apparently few officers believed it would happen.

southern Thailand or north-east Malaya; a Hudson aircraft from the airfield at Kota Bharu had glimpsed them just after noon on 6 December through heavy storm-clouds. A further report at midnight identified twenty-two vessels in the group. At 17.30 on the 7th, there was firm information that a group of warships and transports was moving into Singora, and another to the south. After midnight, news came from the north that 8th Infantry Brigade was being shelled from the sea, and that several ships were anchored directly offshore. Air headquarters ordered Blenheims at Kota Bharu to attack them.

The squadron was soon off the ground. By 02.00 on the 8th, they had found the Japanese and were running in on the transports. General Takumi's headquarters ship, the *Awajisan Maru*, was among those hit, taking a bomb directly through an open hatch. The general, however, had more important matters on his mind. He had heard nothing from Colonel Nasu, commander of the first wave, since their parting at 01.00. There was no sign of the assault craft or ships' boats required to carry the second wave ashore. The wind was increasing. During the commotion and din resulting from the bombing, he was relieved at 02.05 to see a line of assault craft appear and, a few minutes later, to receive a message from the colonel. '01.30 hours. Succeeded in landing but there are many obstacles. Send second wave.'

The boats were already being loaded. General Takumi gave instructions that they were to be got away as quickly as possible, but immediately afterwards he received a message from the naval force commander that they should withdraw to avoid a second air attack. The general insisted that the landings must continue: sea conditions were worsening and any delay would mean that later attempts to land might fail; abandonment of those ashore was out of the question. His firm view prevailed. But soon he was himself obliged to leave the *Awajisan Maru*, which was uncontrollably ablaze. With his tactical headquarters, he set out in assault craft for the beach.

'Many officers and men were killed or wounded,' he wrote later, 'many jumped into the water before the craft had beached and swam ashore. The enemy positions were about 100 yards from the water and we could see that their posts were wired in...' Fortunately for the Japanese, the Indian battalion had only one light battery in support in addition to its six 3-inch mortars. They were unable to meet all the demands for fire from the rifle companies forward and were ineffective against boats still at sea. The most deadly weapons of the Dogras were the medium and light machine-guns located in the concrete posts which swept the barbed wire. In some places there were also minefields.

Colonel Nasu's first wave had come close to a disastrous reverse. Most of the purpose-built steel assault craft had managed to land their passengers without immediate loss, though a few had struck obstacles offshore and overturned, throwing out their complements of whom most, weighed down by weapons and equipment, drowned. But the ships' small boats, made of wood, had frequently been penetrated by machine-gun and rifle fire, causing numerous casualties while they were still on the water – indeed, this fire had persuaded one boatload to make off along the coast.

Those who landed were forced to find shelter on the water's edge. There the strong leadership of the Japanese and the dauntless spirit of the soldiers combined to press the defence. Shell scrapes were begun, trenches developed. Yard by yard, as men took turns at the heavy work, the trenches were extended longitudinally to the edge of the barbed wire, then underneath it. In places, such initiatives were temporarily foiled by exploding mines. Wounded bodies were dragged back down the narrow channels in the sand past grim, sweating men engaged in the development of fire trenches from the main arteries.

By about 03.45, these tactics succeeded in penetrating the central sector of the Dogras, but in the confusion of orders led simply to scattered groups reaching the edge of dense trees and underbrush. To those on the edge of the beach attempting to control events, including the direction of the second and third waves as they came ashore, it seemed that the naval gunfire had also overcome the southern defence posts, though actually they were shelling ground outside the Dogras' sector; the nearest troops to the south were another battalion of the 8th Indian Infantry Brigade covering a beach fifteen miles distant. About a mile from the Dogras' right flank, General Takumi set up his headquarters and concentrated troops and equipment as they arrived. For some hours, however, he was apprehensive that a counter-attack would deny him the time needed to reorganise his force.

Inland, the 8th Brigade commander wished to counter-attack but lacked information as to precisely where the enemy were, apart from those still held by the left and right forward Dogras' positions.

It would probably have paid him to attack quickly to clear the enemy from these, using his third battalion, which was covering Kota Bharu airfield. They were fresh and close at hand. The Dogras' head-quarters could have provided the guides to bring them into a forming-up area and given fire support when they assaulted. As it was, he delayed and then attempted an encirclement across creeks and through uncut foliage in which the movement petered out. The Dogras fought on through the day but it was clear that the Japanese were reconnoitring a way round their southern flank and through their centre. More transports were appearing – the next echelon of the Japanese 18th Division. The airfield at Kota Bharu had been heavily attacked and prematurely abandoned. The brigadier was given permission to withdraw his force behind it that evening.

Meanwhile, after minor misadventures and confusion ashore, the 5th Division under Lieutenant-General Matsui had landed without contest at Singora and Patani. The British command had prepared a special force to pre-empt this invasion but, despite the air reports that it was impending and the authority from London to launch it at his discretion, the commander-in-chief paused until the oppor-tunity had passed. A greater fault was that, apart from preparing bridges for demolition, little had been done to lay out an active defence of this evident line of approach. The commander of the 11th Indian Division was obliged to make a defence in haste. He compounded his difficulties by attempting to cover every yard of a huge sector. The upshot was that his forces were fragmented.

The bridge demolitions close to the frontier delayed the Japanese advance. Rainstorms hindered both sides. But those attacking, not without moments of doubt in the first heated engagements, benefited from their persistence, their refusal to be delayed by main positions commanding roads and their scorn for the weather. The first tanks brought forward from Singora and Patani were used to good effect. The infantry, well supported by the divisional artillery, infiltrated through the rubber plantations. The defenders found themselves dancing to the Japanese tune: their soldiers were moved too frequently, deployed into unknown localities in darkness, subjected in small groups to the noises and loneliness on the edge of jungle, and kept too long on the alert. Too little care was taken to pass information down and up the chain of command. Rumour and fatigue multiplied difficulties. Cohesion was lost. At a crucial moment, the anti-tank screen of the British rearguard failed – the crews were sheltering from the rain, leaving their guns unmanned – and the Japanese, heedless of the downpour, broke through. Seventy-two hours after the first landings, less than six hundred infantry and the ten light tanks of Matsui's 5th Division drove deep into the defences at Jitra, the only fully prepared position in the north, routing two brigades. Japanese losses were fifty men. They captured almost half the first-line transport in the area with guns, munitions, petrol and food. Alor Star with its main and subsidiary airfields was now available to the Japanese 3rd Air Group.

General Matsui's 5th Division was getting the measure of its enemy. Where road-blocks were encountered, tanks or dive-bombers broke them open while the main body of the attacking infantry made outflanking marches through plantations or jungle to get behind the blocking force. Passing through jungle, hacking a path, maintaining a course, was not easy, but they had practised it frequently in their training. General Takumi's force on the east coast, through lacking the armour and weight of the 5th, pressed forward by similar flank marches.

The British were unable to use the sea either to land forces in counter-attacks or, a few minor enterprises apart, for logistics. The two great warships, *Prince of Wales* and *Repulse*, which might otherwise have kept one or other sea flank open for some time, had been sunk on 10 December by air attack. On 9 December Vice-Admiral Sir Tom Phillips, in his flagship *Prince of Wales*, had diverted from his course back to Singapore to investigate a report of new landings midway along the east coast of Malaya. He had expected that air cover would be sent out to him but it was not. At about 11.50 on the morning of the 10th, the stern section of the *Prince of Wales* was ripped open by two torpedoes launched from Japanese naval bombers. The *Repulse* was hit by five. Other aircraft continued to strike the crippled warships which sank before half past one.

The direct result of this catastrophe was that the Japanese were able to use the sea freely on both coasts to carry detachments to the rear of the enemy. Special engineer boat squadrons had been posted to General Yamashita's army for this purpose and they were supplemented by seizure of local fishing craft and ferries. These operations extended the blocking of British supply lines forward and the withdrawal of those in front. The aircraft of the 3rd Air Group were meantime gaining ascendancy in the skies. By

98

Christmas Day, the British III Corps had been pushed over the Perak river and the first of the Japanese Imperial Guards regiments was ordered to cross – a crossing which, astonishingly, was not contested. Twenty-Fifth Army had advanced over 200 miles in a month. On 7 January, a tank company, a battalion of infantry, and a detachment of engineers broke into the British Slim river defences held by two brigades, though these were much depleted. By the end of the month, the British command had been forced out of Malaya into Singapore. General Yamashita was, as it happened, at the limit of his administrative resources but had no intention of biding his time for supplies. On 15 February 1942, the island surrendered after a brief final struggle. Over 130,000 officers and men of the British Imperial forces, including a fresh division recently arrived, had been defeated by an enemy numbering 110,660.

This disastrous opening round of the war in the Far East may be traced to a series of mistaken Allied policies and practices, the upshot of the political and economic climate in the two decades after the First World War. But the military cannot blame the politicians for their own professional errors. There had been good intelligence that the Japanese were training for jungle warfare in Indo-China and on Hainan Island, and that new airfields were being built in southern Indo-China. They had had thirty hours' warning that troop convoys were sailing in their general direction, eight hours' notice that these had turned in to the Kra Isthmus and north-east Malaya. Yet they could not bring themselves to believe that this force was about to batter down their back door.

Then, well in advance of the final crisis, Churchill was warning his chiefs of staff committee on 15 December 1941,

Beware lest troops required for ultimate defence of Singapore Island and fortress are not used up or cut off in Malayan peninsula...

And again on 19th December:

....After naval disasters to British and American sea power in Pacific and Indian Oceans we have no means of preventing continuous landings by Japanese in great strength in Siam and the Malay peninsula... The commander-in-chief should now be told to confine himself to the defence of Johore and Singapore, and that nothing must compete with the maximum defence of Singapore. This should not preclude his employing delaying tactics and demolitions on the way south and making an orderly retreat...

The military commanders did not take up this option even though they had experienced the formidable power of the Japanese on the ground, in the air and at sea. The Jitra position had been broken open by a relative handful of attackers. The risk of sailing the battle-cruiser *Repulse* and the *Prince of Wales*, a battleship only completed earlier in the year, off the east coast of Malaya without air cover was not recognised by the commander-in-chief or his individual service commanders in Singapore. The lessons of the German air attacks on the Home Fleet in the North Sea during the Norwegian expedition had not been learned.

The errors and omissions at strategic level continued at tactical level: huge frontages were allotted to units; the co-ordination of all arms was inept. Only one formation commander, the Australian Major-General Bennett, attempted to ambush the foe, and his success came too late. The field force was by then exhausted, the majority demoralised.

Those who fought at unit level in Malaya have been described as raw and inexperienced. This is not entirely true: many of the regular officers and NCOs had been posted home or to the Middle East, but there were more than enough experienced hands to bring on the talents of those with a year or less of service, and plenty of able young men yearning for greater responsibility.

The fundamental problem was that the troops in Malaya were not trained for jungle warfare. There was no school for cadres, no training manual, because there was no doctrine. There was no separate training office in the General Staff, ranking with the operations, staff duties and intelligence sections, because the senior commanders did not see it as a matter of first importance. Operations in jungle were considered to be impractable. Manoeuvres through plantations incurred the criticism of civil government and, more painfully, payment for damage. A charge sometimes levelled at brigade and higher commanders in Malaya during 1940 and 1941 was that they could only think about armoured warfare while the Japanese concentrated on development of their infantry. As manifested, the opposite was true; the Japanese had worked out a means of combining infantry and light armour effectively in jungle warfare in co-operation with the air force. The British failure was in both anti-armour and counter infantry tactics. During the last weeks of peace, a very few infantry commanding officers had incurred the displeasure of their superiors by adapting their skills comprehensively to jungle fighting and it is not surprising that it was these units which, despite the hazards and fatigue of withdrawal, reached Singapore fit to fight on.

The battle for air superiority was won by the Japanese partly due to the obsolescence of the aircraft assigned to the British Far East Air Force. With the homeland threatened and the Middle East in danger of falling to Germany, it is not surprising that new models were disposed principally to those areas; the Hurricanes which were sent to Singapore were too few and arrived too late to change the outcome of the struggle. But other considerations had influenced the drift of the Far East Air Force into obsolescence. Besides the political notion that the Japanese would be likely to attack Russia before other territories in the Orient, there was also a naval and army view that air power, though important, was not decisive to the outcome of war at sea and on land. For its part, the Royal Air Force here, as elsewhere, continued to believe that its principal role would be in operations largely independent of those on land and at sea, and thus its claims for modern aircraft did not command the insistent support of the other two services. A joint land and air operations room was established belatedly in Singapore but did not involve the navy. And there were still some in positions of importance who assumed that the Japanese lacked the talent to operate fighting aircraft effectively and, indeed, doubted that they could fly aircraft at night or in poor weather. This contributed to the lack of apprehension, when the invasion fleet was sighted, that aircraft in north Malaya might be caught on the ground at any moment.

The root of this outlook was that the Japanese were, after all, Asians, and thus were supposedly incapable of matching the qualities of British leadership, intelligence and skill; little better than the rag, tag and bobtail Chinese Nationalist Army, which they had failed to defeat decisively.* It was a widespread view which pervaded every level of the expatriate community, persuading its membership that if the Japanese came they would soon be defeated. War would not disturb life behind the lines. While battles were raging in north Malaya in the second week of December, a warrant officer drove all the way down to Singapore to collect urgently needed spares for his regiment. He arrived on a Saturday evening and was surprised to find all the lights burning, dinners and dances, as usual, in progress. Reaching the ordnance depot he was refused assistance by a disgruntled duty officer who reminded him that it was the weekend. The depot would not reopen until Monday morning.

So Malaya and Singapore fell. Across the Straits, the invasion of the British Borneo colonies and the Dutch East Indies were in train. Beyond, the United States was struggling to maintain an operational capability in the Philippines. Soon the British Indian Army in Burma and a great mass of Americans and Australians would be learning the lessons of jungle fighting taught so expensively in the opening rounds in the Pacific.

---

* It is an interesting reflection that five years after the war in which the Japanese proved a formidable enemy, the United States sent a small task force as its first contingent to enter the Korean War, confident that its men with their superior education and technology would outmatch the advanced guard of the North Korean People's Army. The force was routed on its first encounter.

# CHAPTER FOURTEEN

# THE FALL OF THE PHILIPPINES

While General Yamashita was supremely confident that he could capture Malaya and Singapore with a force of less than three divisions, his colleague Lieutenant-General Homma Masaharu, was uneasy concerning his instructions to capture the Philippines with a similar body. Homma commanded the Fourteenth Army, like Yamashita's Twenty Fifth a subordinate element of Field-Marshal Count Terauchi's Southern Army Group.

Malaya and Singapore were a single entity. The Philippines comprise eleven sizeable islands amongst a sprawl of some thousands. They extend south to Borneo, north to within a few hundred miles of Taiwan. Singapore lies 1,500 miles to the south-west, but in the north-east Honolulu is 5,000 and San Francisco 7,000 miles distant. During the planning studies in October 1941, the Japanese high command decided that Luzon, the principal and most northerly island, should be taken first. It was within the radii of action of bomber aircraft on Taiwan, though at the limit for escorting fighters, and contained numerous airfields and strips. The main American and Filipino defence force was stationed on the island but the army element would be scattered to deny landings, protect airfields, supplies, workshops and the capital, Manila.

Japanese intelligence was well informed about the United States and Filipino armed forces; they maintained more that one hundred primary agents among the islands, many in industries serving government or defence agencies and a few as domestic servants to government ministers, senior officials and service officers. The only US Army formation in the islands was the Philippine Division under Major-General Jonathan Wainwright, and this was known to be below strength except for its complement of Filipinos.*

---

* These were the Philippine Scouts, raised by the United States when it held the islands as a colony and maintained, after the conferment of commonwealth status on the Philippines in 1934, as the basis of a future national defence force.

Otherwise, ground defence depended upon the ten Filipino divisions raised and trained by General Douglas MacArthur,* to whom overall command of the army, including the army air force, had been passed on 26 July 1941.

The development of the Filipino forces, which included a naval and air component, had been slow under their American instructors. Much of this was due to language difficulties – few Filipinos spoke English, Spanish was declining, and no common language had emerged successfully among the many native tongues. Weapons and equipment were those discarded by the regular United States forces; much had been manufactured before the First World War. There had been some modernisation during 1941, and there were considerable increases in war necessities of all kinds from July onwards. The small United States Army Air Force element was in the process of being built up with modern P-40 fighters and B-17 bombers. Reinforcements began to arrive. Some 6,000 regular officers and men, and intermittently groups of recalled reservists, reached Luzon between July and 7 December. The 4th Marines, 750 strong, were transported to Luzon from Shanghai to help protect the base of the American Asiatic Fleet in Luzon.

The need of the Japanese high command to preserve the secrecy of its attack of Pearl Harbor militated against a near simultaneous landing in the Philippines. The sea passages from Taiwan, the Ryukus, and Palau in the Caroline Islands, the three assembly areas of the Fourteenth Army, were relatively short, but if the whole invasion force put to sea on converging courses from these locations before the attack on Hawaii there could be no doubts about their destination and thus that Japan was about to begin hostilities. Surely, the defences of the Pacific Fleet base would be alerted at once. It was therefore decided that the first strike on Luzon should be by air – airfields and aircraft being pre-eminent targets – and that a number of small groups, ranging from regiment down to company, should land ahead of the main force

* General MacArthur retired from the US Army as chief of staff in 1935, when he became chief military adviser to the Philippine Commonwealth. Despite his political ambitions and connections with the Republican Party, and his age – he was then rising sixty-two – he was the obvious choice to assume command of the United States Army ground and air forces in the Philippines when war with Japan seemed likely.

to seize offshore and coastal airstrips to provide forward fighter bases. The main force would follow after the attack on Pearl Harbor. General Homma agreed final plans at Iwakuni from 13 to 15 November with his colleagues Lieutenant-General Obata Hideyoshi commanding the 5th Air Group, Vice-Admiral Tsukahara commanding the 11th Air Fleet – his fighters had a greater range than those of the army – and Vice-Admiral Takahasi Ibo commanding the 3rd Fleet.

The need for secrecy weighed strongly with General Homma to the extent that the briefing of subordinates was delayed in many cases until after the attack on Pearl Harbor. He was also extremely concerned that his troops would be discovered and attacked at sea by the United States Army Air Force on Luzon; there were continuing reports by Japanese agents of arrivals of modern aircraft on the island. It was clear that the whole American and Filipino defence force would have been mobilised before his main body arrived, yet the plans of Southern Army Group obliged him to land the better part of a brigade on Mindanao and Jolo Islands as part of the overall scheme of invasion of the East Indies. He was not confident that he had sufficient troops for his task.

General Obata had different views. He wished his 5th Air Group aircrew to be familiar with routes and conditions. In the ten days before X-Day, 8 December, formations of bombers and fighters exercised over the Luzon Strait and the South China Sea. These movements were picked up from time to time by one of the two early warning radar stations on Luzon★ and by American naval and army air patrols. They contributed to the apprehensions of the American military and the Philippine government.

With the arrival of the reinforcing P-40s and the B-17s, General MacArthur's confidence in his position had grown. A senior air commander, Major-General Lewis Brereton, had been posted to him early in November bringing, incidentally, a personal letter from General George Marshall, the army chief of staff, which promised an increasing flow of reinforcements and supplies.

'Dick,' MacArthur said to his own chief of staff, Brigadier-

---

★ Seven sets had arrived but crews for only two. As a temporary measure, the air force had established an observer corps, principally postmasters, to report enemy air movements by telephone or direct telegraph to the air defence command.

General Sutherland, 'they are going to give us everything we have asked for.'

The difficulty was that the quantity of goods that the newly fledged American war industries could provide was limited. So was the quality: almost 80 per cent of one delivery of 81 mm mortar ammunition proved to be duds; early batches of artillery fuses were faulty. The numbers of trained reserves in the United States were limited. Still, it was believed in Washington and Manila that there was time to rectify such problems. Some thought the Japanese would attack in February 1942, others, taking account of the monsoon season, opted for April. The president of the Philippines hoped that his country might be regarded as neutral and not attacked at all.

Alarmed by the information drawn from the Japanese diplomatic codes, the United States naval and army departments signalled all principal commanders in the Pacific on 24 November that surprise attacks were a possibility. On the 27th, MacArthur showed his naval colleague, Admiral Hart,* the following:

> Negotiations with the Japanese appear to be terminated to all practical purposes with only the barest possibilities that the Japanese government might come back and offer to continue. Japanese future action unpredictable but hostile action possible at any moment. If hostilities cannot repeat cannot be avoided the United States desires that the Japanese commit the first overt act. This policy should not repeat not be construed as restricting you to a course of action that might jeopardize your defense...

Certain protective measures had been decided on, the most important being the evacuation of the B-17s from Clark Field north of Manila to Del Monte on Mindanao, though seventeen were still at Clark on the night of 7/8 December. It has to be said that one reason at least for their presence was the decision of the 27th Bombardment Group, their owners, to give a party for General

---

* Admiral Thomas C. Hart, commanding the Asiatic Fleet, was neither under General MacArthur nor the commander-in-chief of the Pacific Fleet at Pearl Harbor. He reported directly to the chief of naval operations in Washington.

Brereton before he continued on a wide-ranging tour of the Pacific territories.*

Fog gathered in Taiwan during the night of 7/8 December, persisting into the morning. To General Homma's dismay, the aircraft which were to destroy the enemy's air capability were still in their dispersals, though armed and fuelled for operations. He feared that when they were eventually launched there would be a major air battle from which the American aircraft would be able to retire to distant airfields. Many of the ground targets would by then also be dispersed.

His fears were unnecessary. Although a warning of imminent hostilities sent by General Marshall at the eleventh hour was not despatched to General MacArthur, word quickly reached the various headquarters in Manila that Pearl Harbor had been attacked. The naval commander-in-chief there repeated to Admiral Hart the dismal news he was sending at 08.00 to Washington. 'Air raid on Pearl Harbor. This is no drill.'

Neither Admiral Hart nor his staff, who received the message at 02.30 Philippines time, reported this to General MacArthur's headquarters. An hour passed before an army signalman on night watch happened to hear the news broadcast on a Californian radio programme. He hastened to alert the duty officer. General MacArthur was informed about 03.35, General Brereton at 04.00.

Dawn broke at 06.12 but by that time no alert measures had been implemented. Admiral Hart's ships in harbour remained at anchor. These included twenty-four serviceable submarines; only two of the force complement were patrolling the enemy sea approaches. General MacArthur was incommunicado. When General Brereton attempted to see him at 05.00 hours, the chief of staff, General Sutherland, said that he could not be disturbed. Relationships were not such that Brereton could insist on seeing his commander-in-chief or at least know that he was aware of his request. Brereton wished to despatch immediately a bomber attack against the Taiwan airfields. He ordered Colonel Eubank, commanding the Clark Field B-17s, to bomb up before returning at 07.15 to

---

* General Brereton was later to say that he did not send the remaining B-17s to Del Monte because he was expecting another group from the United States and there was insufficient room for the whole force on a partially developed base. However, some of the crews at the party certainly expected to move to Del Monte in the following week.

Sutherland's office but was again neither admitted to see General MacArthur nor given orders.

Returning to his nearby office, General Brereton received a telephone call from General Arnold, chief of the army air forces in Washington, warning him not to have his aircraft destroyed on the ground as had happened at Pearl Harbor. Instructions were at once sent to Clark Field to put the B-17s into the air without bombs. Fortunately, the earlier order to bomb up had not been acted on; ground and air crews were only just being roused, some with difficulty as a consequence of the previous evening's party.

The pursuit – air-defence – squadrons were now coming to full alert. The radar at Iba indicated that aircraft were approaching, and thirty-six P-40s were sent to investigate. Still unable to see the commander-in-chief, Brereton gave orders shortly after 10.00 for a reconnaissance of the southern Taiwan airfields as soon as possible. What followed between MacArthur, Sutherland and Brereton is not clear; their recollections conflict concerning orders given or withheld throughout this morning, but the result was that at 11.30, when reports began to come in to the air interception centre of approaching aircraft, the B-17s were on the ground at Clark Field refuelling in company with a P-40 squadron. A warning was despatched at 11.45 to Clark as the four other air-defence squadrons were ordered to get into the air.

The approaching aircraft were not those of the Japanese 5th Air Group which had come at 09.30 to bomb ground targets in northern Luzon and departed. It was this force which had been seen on the Iba radar, though they were not found by the American interceptors. Now, the fog having dispersed, 108 Mitsubishi OB-01 bombers of the 11th Air Fleet were arriving to attack the foremost Luzon air bases. They were escorted by eighty-four Mitsubishi A6M2 fighters, 'Zeroes', the most effective fighter in the Pacific. The formation arrived over Clark Field at 12.15, just as the refuelled fighter squadron was readying for take-off. The B-17s were lined up by their squadron buildings, undispersed and unsuspecting; the warning from the interception centre had not been passed on.

The Japanese naval bombers made their attack in two formations from heights above 20,000 feet. The American anti-aircraft guns could not reach this height; their ammunition was old, the fuses corroded. Many shells failed to explode at all. But the Japanese bombs were delivered with accuracy on hangars, barracks, stores and ground transport parks. A long series of explosions began, buildings were shattered or set on fire, men in and out of doors were thrown violently about by blast. Heat and sparks from the fires caught the dry trees and scrub round the airfield, extending the smoke pall. While men were recovering from the initial shock of surprise to spring to the aid of wounded comrades and to man weapons, the second wave began: a low level attack by thirty-four of the Zeroes, taking the aircraft on the ground – only three of the air-defence squadron managed to take off – whose tanks, full of fuel, quickly ignited. Shortly afterwards, a smaller but no less destructive attack was delivered by the 11th Air Fleet on Iba.

Next day, seven Japanese bombers escaped the persistent morning fog on Taiwan to bomb Nichols Field, destroying a number of air-defence aircraft on the ground and important facilities. On the 10th, more than one hundred came again with Zeroes, striking Nichols, Nielson and Del Carmen airfields, ships in Manila Bay and the naval base at Cavite, eight miles south-west of Manila. The shipyard rapidly caught fire. Warehouses, work-shops, the barracks and dispensary, the power-house and a store of 200 torpedoes were destroyed; 500 officers and seamen were casualties. Admiral Hart observed from a rooftop in Manila the dreadful sight of his naval base in flames. As he watched, a signals yeoman brought him a message with the news that the *Prince of Wales* and *Repulse* had been sunk. He decided then that he must withdraw his fleet from the Philippines, leaving only the submarines to operate among the islands. General MacArthur's objection that this would leave him without any means of keeping open the sea lanes for his supply and reinforcement did not make him change his mind. To remain without air cover was to risk total destruction.

An unyielding fog on Taiwan gave the defenders a day of respite on the 11th, but the 5th Air Group devastated the Luzon airfields on the 12th and 13th and ambushed returning American naval patrol bombers. The ability of the remaining handful of B-17s to operate from the Philippines was extremely doubtful and the decision was taken to send them to Australia, from where they could give occasional support using Del Monte as a forward refuelling facility. The surviving fighters, perhaps a dozen or so P-40s and older aircraft, would be kept in action for as long as possible from dispersed, camouflaged sites. Submarines apart, the

Asiatic Fleet retired southward. The ships at sea with reinforcements and ordnance for the Philippines were diverted. The islands stood alone.

The uncharacteristic hesitancy which General MacArthur showed briefly at the outset of attack was quickly set aside. He had had sufficient confidence in the reinforcement and supply programme, and in the late development of the Philippine Army, to set aside the original war plan, which provided in the event of an invasion of the islands for a withdrawal of the garrison to the Bataan peninsula on the northern wing of Manila Bay, there to sit out a defence for up to six months. In its place, he drafted a scheme to conduct an active defence to defeat an invader. Dispositions were made to counter enemy landings on Luzon* while a smaller group of three Filipino divisions was to run down any minor incursions attempted in the area Visayan–Mindanao. All the immense force of his personality and many professional talents as a soldier were directed into readiness for the arrival of the anticipated Japanese invasion. This effort was complemented by that dynamic energy characteristic of the Americans when enthused for a task: stores were combed out, fuel and buildings appropriated; weapons, equipment and vehicles worked or reworked to make good losses or mitigate the absence of items expected in the sea convoys. There was talk of carriers bringing fighter reinforcements to within flying range of the islands and new airstrips were built in the central and southern Philippines to receive them. Contact was established with Australia as the site for an alternative base. Morale was high among the American military. The atmosphere of confidence began to spread among the Filipino divisions, though not among the more perceptive of their instructors.

General Homma's apprehensions were shared by some of his immediate subordinates, including his chief of staff, but these related to weakness of numbers relative to the American forces in the Philippines and the danger that this imbalance might be made worse by losses on passage to the battle area. They respected the United States armed services but judged them to be vulnerable due to soft living, like the British. They had no lack of confidence in the capacity of their own soldiers to defeat them given safe delivery and a firm lodgement.

* The proposal to hold the islands was well received in Washington where the chiefs of staff were co-ordinating a general war plan with the United Kingdom and others under the title 'Rainbow'.

That confidence was the product of their years as regimental officers, an important phase of education in the military virtues. In garrison, the officers lived apart from their men in lodgings among the civil populace but invariably with the barest accommodation. Although that was directly due to scant pay and allowances, these poor circumstances were themselves a reflection of the high command's expectation of simplicity among warriors: 'If you do not make simplicity of life an objective, you will become frivolous and acquire fondness for luxurious and extravagant ways.' It was understood that this would lead to neglect of a responsible attitude to the duty and well-being of subordinates. Contrary to a belief widespread among the British and American forces, Japanese officers were neither aloof from nor persistently brutal to their men. Though striking of inferiors in rank when enraged was not unknown, the superior who did so was widely regarded as having manifested an inability to control his emotions, losing 'face' by the act.

Regimental officers were expected to show a keen interest in those under their command, but this related almost exclusively to their development as soldiers, in identifying potential specialists, bringing on leaders, and encouraging those who had physical or educational difficulties with instruction. It was very much to do with inculcating the outlook of the warrior. An American officer, completing language training in Japan with a military unit in the 1930s, returned to barracks with an infantry battalion one summer afternoon after a march of twenty-five miles in full equipment. When the battalion was dismissed, the company to which he was attached remained on parade to be marched again round the area. At the completion of this additional exercise, as the soldiers made their way to their quarters, the American asked the company commander why he had ordered it. 'I'm just proving to them that they still have lots of "go" and are not nearly so tired as they think they are,' he replied.

Conceivably, this hard lesson might have been taught to the young recruits in the new armies of Nazi Germany, but the attitude manifest in the following must surely be peculiar to the period in Japan. Japanese infantry on manoeuvres in 1936 completed a march of almost thirty miles at 02.00 one morning. The battalion to which a British officer was attached was ordered to patrol extensively within the hour. The officers in his company selected those who were to carry their weary bodies off on these tasks not on the basis of those most fit but to avoid loss of 'face' among those excluded.

The overall system of education and training, working upon deep roots in the Japanese national character, evoked an extraordinary response. Robert Lerquin, a French journalist who accompanied a unit on active service in north-east China in 1937, noted that,

> Repeatedly in the course of the campaign, the men of certain units were impelled by their combative ardour and their desire for hand-to-hand fighting to impose their will on that of their officers; they dragged the officers along with them in an assault, despite evident necessity to wait for a more propitious moment ...Passion controls the nerves of the Japanese soldier, and the warrior in him predominates over the military man.

The emotions of the Japanese Imperial forces had been developed for war. Men would weep when the emperor passed in a railway carriage as they stood by the track waving flags, just as they wept at General Yamashita's conference when briefed to do battle for their sovereign and the land and people he represented. That same passion was manifested, though under control, at the end of a day's work when the officers changed from uniform into kimonos to clean their swords with white silk handkerchiefs, a cloth bound over each owner's mouth so that the breath should not tarnish the blade. None of those present spoke while this sacred task was undertaken. In the same mood, the soldiers stripped and polished their rifles and bayonets. From this mould came the infantrymen and engineers who would hurl themselves into the embrasures of enemy machine-guns, masking the fire with their bodies; the sailor who would drive torpedoes into the hulls of enemy ships without seeking escape; the *kamikaze* pilots ready to fly their aircraft into the decks of the enemy navies.

The groups who landed on Luzon between 10 and 12 December 1941 were, therefore, not only expecting to go into combat but desirous of it. A naval detachment landed on Batan Island* to prepare a fighter strip. On the same day, 10 December, Colonel

* Not to be confused with the peninsula of Bataan on the northern side of Manila Bay.

112

Tanaka with about 800 troops of his 2nd Formosa Regiment*
landed at Aparri and, due to high seas, at Gonzaga on the north
shore of Luzon. Being assailed only from the air, they progressed
sixty miles southward to Tuguegarao over the next two days. Major
Kanno, commanding a detachment from Colonel Tanaka's regiment, landed in the north-west at Viggan through the equally rough
water, though it took two days to set his men ashore. B-17s, P-40s
and P-35s made more serious attacks on this landing – the last
significant US air enterprise before the second series of Japanese air
strikes – but losses did not deter him from sending a reinforced
company to capture the town and airfield at Laoag, fifty miles to
the north. The greater part of a brigade group was landed in the
extreme south of Luzon in the morning of 12 December under
cover of carrier aircraft. By then, landings were in train for Davao
in Mindanao, and Jolo Island, midway between Borneo and
Mindanao.

When Major-General Jonathan Wainwright, commanding the
North Luzon Force of four divisions of the Philippine Army,
learned of the landings at Aparri and Viggan, he believed that they
were feints to disperse his forces. He would not therefore be drawn,
believing, correctly, that a major landing would soon be attempted
in the Lingayen Gulf. This view was supported by General
MacArthur. The bold option of blooding at least one of his
divisions in running down the invaders would probably have been
ruinous in the light of later experience. Another course would have
been to commit the Philippine Scouts to this task, but they were a
precious commodity among the otherwise raw Filipino soldiers.
General Wainwright wanted to fight his force as a body when the
time came. He was also acutely aware that he could not rely on air
support. These considerations illustrate the weakness of the
Philippine command from the outset of operations. Thus Colonel
Tanaka was able without opposition to join up with Major Kanno,
reconstituting his regiment; and the 5th Air Group was able to take
into use the rudimentary airfields of northern Luzon.

General Homma's main force duly appeared on 22 December to
land in the Lingayen Gulf, north of Manila, and at Lamon Bay, to

---

* There were two Formosan Regiments in General Homma's force. The
conscripts were Chinese – Taiwanese – but the officers and some senior non-
commissioned officers were Japanese. They were no less hardy and combative
than the wholly Japanese units in the force.

the south of it. With so many detachments advanced elsewhere, the 48th Division, which led the Lingayen landing, had under its command the balance of the infantry – eight battalions – an armoured reconnaissance regiment and about a hundred tanks, but with substantial artillery. The 16th Division landing at Lamon Bay on Christmas Eve was also under strength – about 7,000 all ranks, less than half of them infantry, the remainder were at Legaspi and Davao. General Homma did not think much of this division's record and saw its role principally as a distraction to the American command.

The landings at Lingayen were chaotic. The sea continued to be extremely rough. The infantry and light artillery managed to get ashore but all were soaked in salt water so there was no radio communication from ship to shore. Four gallant B-17s managed to strike with some effect at the concentration of ships and there was briefly a submarine attack.* For a time General Homma had no idea what was happening to his force. If there had been an immediate counter-attack in strength there would have been serious difficulties, perhaps a major setback in spite of his supremacy in the air and at sea. But there was none. The first wave of his lively and eager soldiers had moved directly from the beach into the action under pre-arranged covering fire from the naval escort force. Dismayed by their vigour, many of those waiting in defence dropped their rifles and fled.

Though they were described as such, in terms of military capability it is misleading to say that General Wainwright had four divisions. Each was small, 7,500 all ranks, weak in artillery and engineers – some divisions had none at all – and was composed of soldiers who had little more than elementary training, non-commissioned officers who had mostly been promoted through two or three ranks in a few months, and officers whose language they understood with great difficulty. In eight days the North Luzon force was pushed back 100 miles, the regiments frequently broken into a disorderly mob until they were reformed by their American instructors. The Japanese advance would have been greater but for the intervention of American artillery – including a number of

---

* There was no joint plan for the operation of submarines during the battle for the Philippines. The submarine force was largely inactive during its later withdrawal to Australian bases.

114

improvised batteries – the presence of American tanks and the Philippine Scouts, including the 26th Cavalry which fought valorously to great effect.

The inability of his greatly superior numbers to contain the Lingayen and southern landings, however, obliged General MacArthur to reconsider his strategy. During the 23 December, he began to throw off remarks about the inevitability of ultimately withdrawing to Bataan, an idea he had previously forbidden with the abandonment of the original war plan. But when the news came from Brigadier-General Parker on Christmas Eve that another and larger force was landing in south Luzon at Lamon Bay – Homma's 16th Division – it was apparent that continuation of an active defence would lead to the defeat of his forces in detail at an accelerating pace. They must revert to the original concept and withdraw with as much ammunition, equipment, fuel, food and as many weapons and spares as they could carry, to Bataan. From that moment on the conduct of the battle was subordinated to this objective. MacArthur took up his headquarters on Corregidor Island in Manila Bay on Christmas Eve. The engineers began work on the construction of defence lines on Bataan, assisted by the troops drawn back day by day to man them.

If nothing else, the dissemination of this policy calmed the troubled minds of the army. There had been the shock of the air attacks and the initial landings in the islands. Rumours had run wild of a fifth column – which the American official historian discounts after exhaustive enquiry – of paratroops landing (there were none), and of huge numbers of enemy where there were few. Commanders high and low quickly came to realise that they were not holding the Japanese, that their lines were being penetrated or outflanked. Almost all news from above or below made them fearful. Increasingly, they fell back when they had been ordered to stand.

Persistent non-compliance with orders accelerates the sense of anxiety in a hard-pressed army, saps confidence in the prospects of recovery, and discourages any motivation for action other than self-preservation. As in Malaya, such an environment stimulated cowardice among men offered the choice between escaping or being killed or abandoned. It broke those who, fighting sturdily for some time, became physically worn and found suddenly that their moral strength was equally exhausted. In the worst of the crisis the battle

115

was sustained by the men commanders value most in any campaign, the 'plain russet-coated captains' and followers who, day by day, soldier on doggedly, men for all seasons. These stalwarts, mostly in small detachments such as the crews of three tanks and a 75mm gun which blocked a Japanese advance for seven hours, were just able to hold the ramshackle structure together until the decision to withdraw to the Bataan peninsula took effect. Then the spirits of many recovered. Notions such as grit and tenacity, responsibility for comrades, the advantage of collective action, were revived. Men who had run in alarm from a sniper were ready to engage in a fire fight to permit the withdrawal of others, holding steadily until they were given the order to fall back themselves. Some in these engagements showed exemplary courage.

In the first week of the new year, the American forces on Luzon were engaged in a series of withdrawal actions, responsive to daily orders despite recurrent emergencies and crises. If the decision to concentrate on Bataan afforded some capacity for initiative it offered little for enterprise. Still, well supported by their remaining artillery and armour, engaging piecemeal the Philippine Division and detachments of the Philippine Scouts, a degree of control was maintained. The Japanese received some shocks in ambush which showed that their ardour could be cooled if they were taken by surprise. A door was held open successfully for the defenders from the south* to pass into Bataan, escaping the columns from Lamon Bay, but General Homma had to revise his ideas about the 16th Division, which had broken some sharp resistance to its progress.

However, this was the least of the adjustments Homma was obliged to make. As the indications grew that the American and Philippine forces were withdrawing to Bataan, the army commander expected that he would be able to bring the campaign to an end quickly; he had had expectations of committing his army to an attenuated operation, running down pockets of enemy forces scattered through mountains and plantations. His chief of staff remarked that the enemy was 'a cat entering a sack'. These views underestimated the constancy of the United States and Filipino soldiers, and the nature of the ground they were defending. Two

---

\* The South Luzon forces had been withdrawn under the inspiring leadership of Major-General Albert M. Jones and Brigadier-General George M. Parker with the aid of a small group of remarkable American and Filipino officers.

considerable mountain features, one behind the other, dominate the Bataan peninsula. On the eastern and western coasts there is some cultivation but in between lies jungle or scrub on rough, rising ground. By the end of February, the defenders had been forced off the first set of mountains but at great cost. The Fourteenth Army had lost a total of 2,700 killed, 4,300 wounded and evacuated. More damaging was the level of sickness: 10,000 were stricken with beri-beri, dysentery, blackwater fever and malaria. The infantry available to fight were reduced to the strength of three battalions. General Homma believed that a strong American counter-attack would be irresistible. The strength was not there, however. Casualties from disease had, similarly, sapped the American and Filipino numbers. The defenders were also seriously short of food and medicines. There was a lull.

In Tokyo, the Japanese high command was dissatisfied with General Homma's performance but decided not to disgrace the army by removing him*. Its displeasure was made clear by dismissing his chief of staff and several other senior members of his headquarters. But an end to the fighting would only be brought about by reinforcing the Fourteenth Army. The 4th Division was sent from Shanghai – 'the worst equipped' in the Japanese Army in Homma's view – a strong detachment from the 21st Division *en route* to Indo-China, and a considerable number of individual reinforcements. The artillery was substantially strengthened. The tactical air force, much of which had been withdrawn on the assumption that the campaign was almost over, was sent the 22nd Air Brigade.

By the beginning of April 1942, the Japanese Army had completed reorganisation and an intensive training programme. Plans were ready to break in through the mountainous centre while feinting on the flanks. On the 3rd, Good Friday, between 10.00 and 15.00, a colossal bombardment by artillery and aircraft fell upon the American defences.

General MacArthur had been ordered to leave Corregidor in March and had successfully completed a perilous escape with his wife and son to Australia. His successor in the Philippines was General Wainwright. The commander on Bataan was Major-

---

* Homma was virtually dismissed at the conclusion of the Philippines campaign. Recalled to Japan, he was unemployed throughout the remainder of the war.

General Edward P. King Jr, whose force, unlike the Japanese, had had no reinforcements or new supplies. It was daily weakening physically. The opening bombardment assisted the initial assault of the Japanese offensive but did not rout the defenders. An American counter-attack on the 6th recovered some of the features lost but failed at others. A wedge had been driven between the two skeleton 'corps' in defence. They were doomed. On 9 April, General King surrendered 78,000 men to General Homma. Some 2,000 escaped to the island of Corregidor which fought on for a further month. On 9 June, resistance ceased by order in the southern islands.

'Your high command has come to an end,' General Homma informed General Wainwright. 'You are now a prisoner-of-war.'

He had become a prisoner among the hundreds of thousands taken in the Philippines, the Dutch East Indies, Hong Kong, Malaya and Singapore – a person of no account among his captors, subjected to Draconian discipline and privation and continually at risk of torture and death; the fate of many of the prisoners under the Japanese control. The Asian peoples in the countries occupied were also to feel the bite of the conqueror. Such were the consequences of long years of isolationism by the United States of America, of failure – as in the democracies of Europe – to meet the demands of defence, the responsibilities of nationhood: a public and humiliating thrashing, and the sacrifice of important outposts in the opening rounds of war.

# PART III

---

# The Shape of Wars to Come

# CHAPTER FIFTEEN

# HOT WAR INTO COLD WAR

At last, almost six years after Germany invaded Poland in 1939 and three and a half years after Japan attacked Pearl Harbor, the Second World War came to an end. During the greater part of those years, the two aggressors had controlled vast tracts of territory to which they had no title and whose people objected to their presence. They had drawn from them food, fuel, raw materials, manufactures and labour at prices hugely favourable to themselves. They had rooted out those who opposed them potentially or actually and, in Europe, those who offended them racially. They took and murdered hostages at will. Physical torture was a customary part of their interrogation of suspects.

The arbitrary incorporation of certain European nations of 'pure' Aryan stock into the Third *Reich* conferred no favours on their citizens, only penalties. For example, a Norwegian caught escaping across the North Sea by boat was charged with treason. He was judged to be deserting from a part of the greater German state, of which he had been made a member and to which perforce he therefore had obligations of duty in time of war. Sometimes the sentence for this offence was death. Otherwise it was condemnation to slavery; the victim's name was erased from all records and a number substituted as identification of a unit of labour. This was the policy of *Nacht und Nebel* (night and mist). The prospectus of liberation from colonialism in the Japanese Greater East Asia Co-Prosperity Sphere was no less false. As Gibbon wrote of other times, 'The increase of taxes, which were drawn away by a distant sovereign, and a general resumption of the patrimony of crown lands, soon dispelled the public joy,' if indeed there had been any joy. The ruthless and arrogant behaviour of the Japanese forces from the outset of their arrival in Malaya and the Philippines had not suggested benevolence to those being 'freed from colonial rule'.

The myth has grown since the war of an immediate collective rejection of their conquerors by each proud nation. The fact is that for months – in some cases years – there was no resistance of note to the conquerors' arbitrary government. The majority of the peoples whose countries were occupied were at first shocked by the event and then systematically terrorised by professionals in counter-intelligence and repression. This was the means by which peoples were kept under control by relatively small numbers of occupation forces, amongst whom worked an even smaller number of experienced security agents aided by a handful of opportunists or broken patriots.

Gradually, patriotism, religious, political or other personal philosophy, singly or collectively stimulated men and women to fight back. It was not easy. Many citizens who loathed the occupying power and its works were none the less opposed to espionage, sabotage or insurgency against them because they feared reprisals. But this apprehension diminished as it became evident that, however well they behaved, murder, torture, imprisonment or enslavement persisted as a matter of policy. Then, as time passed, the news broadcast from the portions of the world still free, received on forbidden channels, suggested that Germany and Japan would be defeated. The notion grew that internal action might hasten that defeat. In many different ways, aided after early errors and omissions by their allies overseas, resistance movements came to life and prospered in each of the occupied countries.

A few fielded active fighting forces – Tito's partisans, for example, which drew in patriots of many persuasions under the Communist banner to tie down an increasing number of German divisions. Others, such as the Viet Minh, followed the example of Mao's forces in China, skirmishing with the Japanese but biding time and husbanding military supplies in readiness for the struggle for national power when the war had been won on distant battlefields. Irrespective of size, the activities of the resistance on whatever scale caused casualties as in conventional war. As in war, they inflicted death and suffering on the civil populace among whom their actions were joined.

At length the weight of men and material, the late developed skill and hardiness in battle of the United States, the British Common-wealth and the detachments large and small of the peoples allied to their struggle, united with the patriotic masses of Russia to overpower Hitler's forces. Though it suited the professional pride of some of the *Wehrmacht*'s leadership to assert that, but for the errors of Hitler's generalship, they would have triumphed in Russia or Normandy, the fact was clear to most that other strategies would at best have simply delayed the same outcome, the defeat of Germany's armed forces on sea, land, and in the air. There was not the slightest basis in 1945 for the legend of 1918, an undefeated army in the field betrayed by political weakness on the home front. When the end came, the remnant of the *Wehrmacht* was fighting in the homeland. On this occasion, it was the sovereign and supreme commander in Berlin who believed that his forces had failed him.

At length, as the Japanese nation was being prepared by General Tojo's government to fight *en masse* for the home islands, the atom bombs fell on Hiroshima and Nagasaki, persuading a sufficient number of the Japanese elder statesmen to support the emperor's view that the time had come to surrender. Among the allied servicemen and their families, among the peoples longing for liberation, no hands were wrung over the damage and suffering wrought by nuclear weapons in the two luckless cities. No lofty view was taken by those committed to recovering the residual territories occupied by Japan and, ultimately, the heartland of Japan itself, that this awesome power must be put back in the box. And that they should, as a matter of moral duty, bring the war to an end with conventional weapons, no matter how many months were added to the term of hostilities, no matter how many more of their number would become casualties. They were too close to the years of occupation, air raids of an increasingly destructive and indiscriminate nature – albeit with high explosive – and the experience of battle. They did not need to ask what form the fighting for Japan would take. Events at Guadalcanal, Tarawa, in Burma and Papua-New Guinea among a host of operations provided the information. The atom bomb brought them a remission from that prospective duty. Paradoxically, it restored peace.

So the victory bells rang.

Within a matter of weeks, the armed forces of the West began demobilisation. It was not simply the sending home of the veterans while the youth conscripted to the great training machines developed in war took their place, man for man. It was a demobilisation in real terms on a grand scale. For whilst there was a need to maintain forces stronger than those required in a settled world – for example, to occupy enemy territory pending peace treaties – there was no requirement to maintain the hosts, weapons, hulls, wheels, tracks, airframes and other equipment disposed for war. The United States went so far as to destroy or abandon quantities of aircraft and other war equipment on many overseas sites. On distant tropical islands, the skeletons of aircraft, stores and huts, the broken remnant of runways, moulder still, overgrown with secondary jungle.

In Russia and throughout its areas of occupation, it was Stalin's policy to do none of these things. While demobilising a number of men with long service, he maintained a full war fighting capability. Whatsoever territory he had under the occupation of the Red Army, he intended wherever possible to hold. Whatsoever peoples he might bring under his influence, he sought to intimidate.

Thus the Baltic states – Lithuania, Latvia and Estonia – had no prospect of resuming independent status. The governments of Czechoslovakia and Poland were by different processes brought to the same end: complete subservience to the Soviet Union. Attempts were made to bring Austria wholly under Russian control. Democracy was denied to Hungary, Bulgaria and Rumania. Jugoslavia was subjected to intense pressure to accept Stalin's fiat. The Draconian regime of Enver Hoxha was bolstered in Albania. The EAM ELAS field force was supported in its efforts to seize power in Greece. Finland was saved from becoming a Soviet Socialist Republic by America, Britain and France. Norway was reminded that it was a close neighbour of Russia; the revision of the Spitzbergen Treaty* and the cession of Bear Island to the Soviet Union was strongly pressed upon the Norwegian government in exile by Stalin in 1944, and again in 1945. Much was made of the withdrawal, some time after the end of the war, of the Red Army from Norwegian and Danish provinces, as if it were a special favour rather than what was owed to these sovereign states, allies in the war. Denmark was aware of repeated Russian claims on territories controlling the Baltic exits and received a warning related to these. The Soviet vice-minister for foreign affairs remarked to the Danish ambassador in Moscow in 1945:

* The treaty of 1920 signed by numerous powers gave prospecting and mining rights to many of them but acknowledged Norway's sovereignty in the archipelago. Stalin wished to replace this by a Russo-Norwegian condominium.

We have certain information which indicates that the Danish politicians view Denmark as a British area of interest and thus a British/American military area. We have to object very strongly against such misconceptions. We must remind you that after this war Denmark will be the direct neighbour of the Soviet Union, and that we no longer have any competitors in the Baltic. We hope Denmark will understand this.

These manifestations of a new threat to peace in Europe added to the many difficulties of a continent partly ruined and much impoverished by war. The United States had offered generous financial aid to all concerned in 1947 under what came to be known as the Marshall Plan. It was accepted readily by the democratic states but refused by Stalin for Russia and the territories he controlled.* By the beginning of 1948, however, it was becoming apparent to Ernest Bevin, foreign secretary of the United Kingdom, that the economic recovery being effected painfully might soon be threatened from behind the 'iron curtain' interposed between eastern and western Europe. In February, as he had feared, the remnant of democratic government in Czechoslovakia was destroyed in a *coup* engineered by the Russians. In the same week, the president of Finland was being urged to complete a pact of friendship and military alliance on the lines of those recently concluded with Hungary and Rumania. Early in March, the Norwegian foreign minister told the British ambassador that his government had information that they, too, had been advised to expect a similar approach from Moscow.

If nothing else had been learned by the European democracies from the events leading up to the Second World War it was that the absence of a strong defensive alliance tempted an aggressor to pick off nations individually. Bevin was already drawing together France, Belgium, Luxembourg, the Netherlands and the United Kingdom – the Brussels Conference – in a mutual defence treaty, but he recognised that this would be inadequate to cope with a Russian move against Norway. Thus he wrote on 11 March to the American secretary of state, George Marshall:

---

* Prior to the *coup* in February 1948, which finally deprived Czechoslovakia of any independence in foreign affairs, its government accepted the principle of Marshall Aid. In 1948, it rejected it on Stalin's order.

...Two serious threats may thus arise shortly: the strategic threat involved in the extension of the Russian sphere of influence to the Atlantic; and the political threat to destroy all efforts to build up a Western union...the most effective steps would be to take very early steps, before Norway goes under, to conclude under Article 51 of the charter of the UN a regional Atlantic Approaches Pact of Mutual Assistance in which all countries directly threatened by a Russian move to the Atlantic could participate, for example, US, UK, Canada, Eire, Iceland, Norway, Denmark, Portugal, France (and Spain, when it has a democratic regime)...We could at once inspire the necessary confidence to consolidate the West against Soviet infiltration and at the same time inspire the Soviet Government with enough respect for the West to remove temptation from them and so ensure a long period of peace. The alternative is to repeat our experience with Hitler and to witness helplessly the slow deterioration of our position, until we are forced in much less favourable circumstances to resort to war in order to defend our lives and liberty...

In later years, when periodic *jalousie de métier* or Washington follies have stimulated hostility for the United States in Europe, the myth has been revived that the Americans forced their presence politically and militarily in the wake of economic aid upon western Europe, even though the national public records show that the contrary is true. No doubt it is also true that they came in a clear perception of their own interest. But it was national interest which drew in all those who helped to foster and ultimately join the Atlantic Alliance following Bevin's message to George Marshall. The education of the United States in international politics had been developed by war across the Atlantic and in the Pacific, and heightened by persistent Russian chicanery and brutality in the immediately following years. If its people found it difficult to focus on the threat of encroachment on Norway and Denmark in the first half of 1948, or the intricacies of a political settlement for Germany, they could see very plainly Stalin's arbitrary disregard for agreements developing over Berlin where, from March onwards, the access which France, the United Kingdom and United States had by right through East Germany was progressively denied. Having taken, as it were, a half-pace back from peacetime alliances in 1945, the government in Washington was uncertain as to what it should do.

'Will not Russian restrictions be added to one by one which eventually would make our position untenable unless we were prepared to threaten or actually start a war to remove these restrictions?' General Omar Bradley, chief of the US Army Staff, signalled on 10 April to General Lucius Clay, military governor of the US occupation zone in Germany: 'Here we doubt our people are prepared to start a war in order to maintain ourselves in Berlin and Vienna.... If you agree, should we now be planning how to avoid this development and under what conditions, say, for example setting up Trizonia* with capital at Frankfurt, we might ourselves announce withdrawal and minimise loss of prestige rather than being forced out by threat?'

Although General Clay had come to believe that Stalin might be ready to have his way by force of arms in Europe – not simply over Berlin – he did not believe that this was his immediate intention. Clay proposed that they should hold fast, if necessary until they were forced out of Germany. Domestic politics did not make it easy for the American president to make such a decision but he took the military governor's advice and, with his allies, declined to withdraw. Press, radio and newsreel coverage of the Berlin situation, and the subsequent successful airlift of supplies into the city, with an associated illumination of the Communist tyranny which had replaced that of the National Socialists in East Germany, continued the process of reminding Americans that they could not with impunity return to isolating themselves from the world. Indeed, they were educated almost daily in this fateful year that, like it or not, the United States was involved in the future of world stability and security not only in northern, central and western Europe but in other areas such as Austria and Italy, Greece and Palestine, even in Kashmir.

Thus the American people, who had already shown themselves ready to support the United Nations Organisation where once they had spurned the League of Nations, were shortly persuaded by events in Europe to join a politico-military alliance to deter war in the old continent. Isolationism, toyed with by Republicans in the aftermath of war, was, for the time being at any rate, dead.

* Trizonia – combination of the French, UK and US zones as an economic unit. The British and US were already running a bi-zonal arrangement.

# CHAPTER SIXTEEN

# A DEFENSIVE ALLIANCE: A TREATY
# OF CONVENIENCE

The North Atlantic Treaty came into force on 24 August 1949. Like the Brussels Treaty it was purely defensive in scope, binding its signatories to mutual defence; that is, an attack upon any one of them would be taken as an attack upon all. There were twelve founder members, Belgium, Canada, Denmark, France, Iceland, Italy, Luxembourg, the Netherlands, Norway, Portugal, the United Kingdom and the United States.*

Eire had opted out. Iceland had agreed to join but had no armed forces to contribute, no intention of raising any from its tiny populace, and took the decision to join only after the failure of a mooted Scandinavian defence union with Denmark, Norway and Sweden. This had foundered, principally because Sweden would not join any alliance showing the least partiality for the Eastern or Western camps, and Norway and Denmark believed that there would have to be some understanding with the West. Norway had been heartened by Finland's success in retaining the essentials of independence in the 'treaty of friendship and defence' it was obliged to enter with the Soviet Union. Even so, the Norwegian government and people were aware that the kingdom was now an immediate neighbour of Russia in the far north[†] and that Stalin had relinquished none of his claims upon it. The German invasion in April 1940 had make it clear that they could no longer depend for their security upon an old-style affirmation and practice of neutrality in disputes between the stronger powers. Lacking the populace or finances to hold off alone a powerful predator, it was

---

* Greece and Turkey acceded to the treaty in 1952, the Federal Republic of Germany in 1955 and Spain in 1982.
† Finland ceded Petsamo to Russia in 1945.

clear that they needed to join together with friends in some form of defence association. They trod carefully and deliberately as the options were weighed, giving to Russia no reasonable cause for offence. But, like Hitler, Stalin needed no reasonable cause other than the narrowest self-interest to engage in the intimidation of neighbours. When the *Storting*, the national assembly in Oslo, debated the proposal to join NATO, Stalin misjudged the Norwegian mettle. He rattled his sabre. Until that event, the outcome was uncertain. Put under external pressure, the representatives of these sturdily independent people, less than four million in number, voted with one exception to become a member of NATO.

The Soviet Union responded to the accomplishment of the Atlantic Treaty in a manner that was then novel but was later to be repeated: it conducted a grand political campaign involving itself, its satellites in eastern Europe, and the Communist parties in all the democracies. To these were joined the protests of a variety of specially formed organisations, some openly led by members of the international Communist movement, some by those who were not. Typical of the former was the International Committee of Intellectuals for Peace which arranged a series of meetings in cities throughout the world, beginning in Paris in April 1949. From this developed the World Peace Committee. The latter included the World Federation of Trade Unions, the World Federation of Democratic Youth and the Women's International Democratic Federation. A spurious popular legitimacy was given to these bodies whose membership was described as 'national', with national delegacy being attributed to those whose speeches were quoted in the many reports of proceedings and pamphlets published. There was no shortage of money in underpinning the many expenses involved, though precisely where it came from was not easy to identify. Public opinion in the democracies was to be informed that the mass of the people, 'the peace-loving peoples of the world', were joining together to protest against the formation of NATO, which endangered peace. The implication that those opposed to the 'peace-loving peoples' were essentially warmongers was not neglected. Sitters on the fence were reckoned to be associate warmongers. Some of the literature articulated very specifically that the danger arose because NATO was 'aggressive' and threatened the Soviet Union.

In many democratic countries the campaign succeeded in convincing elements of the public who had no connection with the Communist Party that the formation of a defensive alliance by the Atlantic powers made war more likely because it was 'provocative', likely to persuade the Soviet Union to rearm. National and local peace committees were formed with the aim of persuading others to this view and to work towards a mass movement to persuade politicians that NATO should be disbanded. The public were not persuaded. The campaign failed. It is probable that this was due as much as anything to a lack of popular interest in defence matters in the democracies; but an important if not the prime reason for failure was that the arguments of the 'peace movement' were false.

The greatest falsehood was that NATO with its collective forces was stronger than the Soviet Union. It was manifest that the reverse was true. The United States possessed nuclear weapons but Russia had by 1949 developed its own. The United States, the United Kingdom and France could muster between them a total of twelve effective divisions for European defence, with the other members perhaps eighteen. Russia alone had fifty divisions under arms at full strength on or close behind its western frontiers. This balance scarcely imperilled the Soviet Union and offered no 'provocation'. When, in the following year, 1950, Stalin provided the armaments for Kim Il-sung's invasion of South Korea, the United States was unable to take part effectively in the United Nations counter-operations until it had called up a considerable number of its reserves. To send one full brigade to Korea the United Kingdom had to recall a fifth of its trained reserve, almost half its infantry reserve and, much against the inclination of the governing party, to extend its term of conscription from eighteen months to two years. There was the same weakness in air potential relative to the Russians, and an even greater weakness in war stocks. It was only at sea that the number and range of warships favoured the NATO membership, but these were distributed across the oceans of the world.

These facts were not precisely assimilated widely but the gist percolated through to people who glanced through newspapers and listened to the radio news daily, or perhaps saw the newsreels at the local movies once a week. They appeared to support other manifestations previously noted: for example, the death in sinister circumstances, in March 1948, of Jan Masaryk, long-standing foreign minister of the freely elected government of Czechoslovkia, a consequence of the Communists' seizure of power in Prague; or the blockade of land access to Berlin by the Russians during 1948–9. These were events bearing the stamp of aggression and dictatorship. By 1950, Marshal Stalin was no longer seen as 'Uncle Joe', the canny wartime ally, but as a cunning and rapacious tyrant. It was not difficult to believe the view widely expressed by governments, parliamentarians, diplomatists and political commentators that Stalin was the regulator, if not the instigator, of the Korean War. It is not enough to say that the public view was formed over the period by a gutter press owned by right-wing newspaper and radio interests in cahoots with cynical politicians. Contrary views were also freely published, and not simply those of the Marxist Left.* These views did not carry.

The peace campaign in Germany was linked with the question of German reunification. In this context, it was argued more credibly that the Soviet Union, which had suffered so much as a consequence of Hitler's invasion, had every right to fear the revival of German politico-military power and so wished to ensure that the final restoration of sovereignty to its former enemy should be dependent on safeguards. All the Russian proposals, however, were directed towards the creation of a weak state vulnerable to a takeover by the strong Communist organisation nurtured in the Eastern zone. The three Western allies, the US, UK and France, were acutely aware of the danger. From the moment of Stalin's refusal of Marshall Aid for the Eastern zone of occupation, the three had begun to accept what the majority of the people of western Germany wished for, separate states in west and east until a strong democracy had been established in the former with the necessary authority and power to negotiate union itself. Stalin countered this with the accusation that such a plan was simply a means of creating a new German military power as a tool of the Western allies. It was due to his determination to resist a settlement for Germany that he had withdrawn his representative from the allied control council in Berlin and blockaded the city to create a crisis, suggesting a risk of hostilities to frighten the three allied governments into abandonment of their tenure in the city, a first step towards abandonment of

---

* See, for example, the articles in the *New Statesman* during February 1948, including two despatches from Prague by R.H.S. Crossman.

their policy for the reunion of the German people. When it failed, he made haste to consolidate his hold on East Germany and carried to completion the extensive purges of governments and communist parties in the other satellites, notably Poland, Hungary and Bulgaria.

Actually, it was the French government and nation which believed it had most to fear in the restoration of German sovereignty. A spectre of right-wing German militarism undoubtedly caused anxiety in France, but so did the prospect of Germany united under a Communist government controlled by Russia. The Communist Party in France had come close to power in 1947. Some believed – certainly members of the interior ministry – that Stalin had given instructions to the party leader, Maurice Thorez, to create conditions for a *coup*. Flying squads of militants had been formed to exacerbate the effects of a general strike; but the party lost the support of blue collar workers. By 1949, the political structure was more stable. Given a choice of something bad or something worse, the creation of the Federal Republic of Germany in the three allied zones of occupation was accepted by the French government. But the re-establishment of armed forces in the West German state, with a view to strengthening the NATO defence potential,* did not attract French support. A member of the Gaullist Party remarked at one of the discussions of the subject in 1950, 'We have been here before. America gave us guarantees at Versailles and reneged. Britain gave us guarantees but couldn't honour them. Germany made promises but Hitler broke them. Why should we risk all this again?'

Eighteen months after the signing of the Atlantic Treaty in April 1949, and a year after it came into effect, the NATO military arm was still a frail body without a head as the United States secretary of state, Dean Acheson, met his colleagues, Ernest Bevin and Robert Schumann of France, in New York on 15 September 1950. Acheson sent this message to President Truman after two days of futile discussion:

> I asked for and obtained a private conference attended by only me, Bevin and Schumann and our three High Commissioners [in

---

* The demands of the Korean War for American and British forces had further weakened NATO strength in Europe. German manpower was the only source of reinforcement.

the Federal Republic of Germany]. The purpose of the talk was to get away from minor difficulties...I pointed out that you had been able to bring about a complete revolution in American foreign policy, based upon the realities of the international situation. We had prepared to take steps which were absolutely unprecedented in our history, to place substantial forces in Europe, to put these forces into an integrated force for the defense of Europe, to agree to a command structure, to agree to a Supreme Commander, to join in a program for integrating European production, to take far-reaching steps in the financial field, but all based upon the expectation that others would do their part, and that the entire scheme would result in the creation of such power that chances of peace would be immeasurably improved; and, if contrary to our hopes and belief war should come, we had a first-class chance to win it. I went on to say that this involved a defense in Europe as far to the east as possible and that such a defense was not possible without facing squarely and deciding wisely the question of German participation. I pointed out that in our discussions the British and French had been prepared to accept what we offered, had been reticent about their own contributions; and had flatly refused to face in any way the question of German participation. I, therefore, wanted to talk about this question with the gloves off and see exactly where we stood.

The ensuing discussions brought out very clearly two fundamental facts. The first was that Bevin, who really agreed with me, had been put under wraps by his government and was not permitted to say anything. This grows out of the current debate in the House of Commons on this very subject, in which the Labour Government has a pathological fear of Churchill and does not dare say anything for fear that it will leak to the American press and be used by Churchill in the debate. I hope this situation is not permanent and may clear up in the near future.

On the part of Schumann the difficulty was deeper. His attitude was that he was not able or willing, as the spokesman of his government, to take any decision even on principle in regard to German participation until the forces of the Allies had been so strengthened in Europe that the French Government could face the psychological reaction to the creation of German armed force. . . . In the [North Atlantic] Council meetings I have already been assured of vigorous support from the smaller European countries. . . It may be that we shall have to have further meetings . . .

Not all the 'smaller European countries' were quite as enthusiastic about German armed forces as Mr Acheson thought. Norway, Denmark and Portugal had distinct reservations. But these were gradually overcome with those of France by American promises to fill out its own contribution as soon as the Korean War came to an end, and to assist France financially in the re-equipment and expansion of its own armed forces. None contested the appointment of an American officer as supreme Allied commander in Europe. It was accepted as reasonable that the United States would not pass responsibility to any other nationality to operate nuclear weapons if such an extremity arose. General Eisenhower was the first incumbent, assured of a welcome due to his high reputation as supreme commander of the Allied forces in north-west Europe in 1944–5. Though he came back to a command that was greater geographically, it was feeble in numbers, declining in quality of arms and equipment and short of finance. In the two years of his term as NATO's military chief in Europe before he returned to run for presidential office, he spent much of his time touring the capitals of his European allies, encouraging and persuading governments to do more than they proposed. At the end of that period, the elements of a command network were in place, though lacking many essential communications. When he came to say goodbye to his British subordinate commanding the northern army group he remarked, 'I wish I had been able to get you all the new radio and telephone equipment you need for your headquarters. And I don't know how you will get by in the meantime.'

'Oh, don't worry,' said the British general. 'I've solved the matter temporarily. My aide keeps his pockets full of 10 *pfennig* pieces and when I want to talk outside the British network we use the German public telephone-box outside the headquarters.'

At the foundation of NATO, it was the intention over succeeding years to match, though not to exceed, the strength of the Soviet field forces both in active and reserve divisions. The potential of West Germany, then approaching sovereignty as the Federal

Republic of Germany, would be realised to match the armed forces being raised in East Germany by the Soviet Union and to mitigate the overall weakness. Britain pledged itself to increase its numbers to seven divisions for Europe – though it has never managed to man and equip more than four. Even the United States at a peak of wealth was then and later unable to maintain more than thirteen active divisions at home and abroad. Hence the adoption of the 'tripwire' concept: small numbers of conventional forces would man the frontier zones; if they were attacked, nuclear weapons would be used against the aggressor.

If they were attacked... This aspect raises another important consideration. For those who, in branding NATO as aggressive, maliciously implied or mistakenly assumed the superior strength of its forces, there was essentially a second assumption: the will of the member governments to carry out the act of aggression. But the alliance was pledged only to defend itself; each government laid that condition before its parliament. The parliaments accepted alliance on those terms alone. All plans made by the three supreme commanders – of the Atlantic, of the Channel, of Europe – were to be approved by the governments of the nations concerned. All were to be of a defensive nature: hostilities should begin only when a clear act of aggression had occurred against the membership. From the beginning, the forces were committed to the inherent disadvantages of the defender, pre-eminently, loss of initiative and vulnerability to surprise. Choice of time and place of offensive action and the option of surprise would lie with the Soviet Union. NATO, with weaker forces, would be obliged to man all frontiers.

Slowly the military arm of NATO began to assume an identity beyond standing groups of staff officers. The long delay in creating a loose collection of forces was due to the fact that the alliance was a partnership of equal nation states. For, although members were not equal physically in size of population, or in financial and industrial base, each, from the United States to Luxembourg, retained its independence, taking its own initiatives and making its own decisions in support or otherwise of policies proposed – often more of a hostage to internal political pressures than to those of its allies.

Such considerations did not apply in the formation of the Warsaw Pact at the end of 1955. Several theories have been offered as to the reason for this development. Those attending the Moscow

Conference of 29 November–2 December 1954 – Albania, Bulgaria, Czechoslovakia, East Germany, Hungary, Poland, Rumania and the Soviet Union – declared that it was a response to the agreements reached in London and Paris immediately beforehand to admit the Federal Republic of Germany to NATO. This does not seem to be the whole truth.

In Stalin's time, there was no need of any additional apparatus for command in war and direction in peace of the satellite forces. His power was absolute. But when Stalin died in February 1953, there was a marginal loosening of the reins. Officially, the Eastern occupation zone of Germany had no armed forces while the future of the German state remained unsettled, but militia had been formed in 1945 under the guise of police,* expanding through 'alert' units in 1948 – fully armed infantry – to a force of all arms in 1949. With the creation of a nominally independent state, the German Democratic Republic, there was no further need for pretence. Comprehensive armed forces could be manifested as part of the apparatus of sovereignty. But the Soviet Union then ceased to be an occupying power and it needed justification for the continuing presence of its land and air forces on East German soil. American, Belgian, British, Canadian and French soldiers and airmen were stationed in West Germany under the Atlantic Treaty, so the Warsaw Pact authenticated the presence of the Red Army.[†] It provided also for the organisation of joint manoeuvres.

Otherwise, little else was changed. Operational command remained in Moscow within the Soviet General Staff. The programme for the design, research, development and manufacture of the entire range of war equipment and the allocation of raw materials and other resources continued to be made by the Soviet Union. The forces of the Warsaw Pact were thus able to enjoy the advantages of a common pattern in every form of weapon and equipment, free from the costly competition within NATO, in which nations vie with one another to sell their own designs in tanks, artillery, aircraft

---

* As agreed at the Yalta Conference, the non-military police forces in the three Western zones of occupation were decentralised, principally to municipal establishments. In October 1945, under the arrangements of the Soviet Union, the police in the Eastern zone were armed and centralised under the regional (*Länder*) governments, and in December under the interior minister. This was a gross violation of the inter-allied agreement.

† The term 'Red Army' in the Soviet Union covers all armed services.

(including helicopters), warships, and the ammunition varieties required in each service. There was no need to negotiate operational concepts, common operating procedures or communications systems, or to wrangle on standardisation boards. All conformed to the Russian pattern.

All conformed, too, to the offensive character of the Red Army on land and in the air. Its structure, though modernised progressively, had not essentially changed since the armistice in 1945. It was organised and equipped for offensive operations. For example, its land forces enjoyed transport and supply echelons capable of supporting the fighting elements in a campaign extending to the extremities of western Europe. The Russian allies were not directed to produce contingents modelled on this capability but to complement it.

Within the Red Army, the Russian Navy in 1945 was not capable of maritime offence. By the time the Warsaw Pact was formed, however, it was evident that a huge programme of naval armament was in process. The appearance of the new cruiser *Sverdlov* at the British coronation review in June 1953 was an early and surprising sign of it. The pre-war concept of an ocean-going fleet as an instrument of international political power had been resuscitated.* The result was a progressive expansion to four fleets – the Northern, Far Eastern, Baltic and Black Sea commands, to the latter two of which neighbouring members of the Warsaw Pact were to contribute.

Taking no account of this offensive capability overall, of which Stalin had reminded other nations quite openly when it had suited him, the Warsaw Pact was launched with a propaganda campaign which stressed that it gathered together states against external menace – NATO and a rearmed Germany being specifically mentioned as potential invaders of the homelands of those concerned – without infringing the independence of any of the signatories. Some of them may have believed the first of these statements. Shortly all knew that the second was false. Within a matter of months Russian troops in Hungary put down the popular uprising against the government.

---

* The plan made by Admiral Kuznetsov, accepted in principle by the *Politburo* in 1928, provided for the construction of 3 battleships, 2 battle-cruisers, 14 cruisers, 82 destroyers and 279 submarines among a total of 533 warships. Post war, the programme was revised and carried forward by Admiral Gorshkov.

Albania is the only state which has escaped wholly from its obligations to the pact. It withdrew in March 1961, perhaps to the relief of the other members. An American military attaché in Paris twitted his Russian colleague on the loss of an ally on the day that the withdrawal became known.

'We don't need them,' the Russian replied. 'You can have them if you like.'

'We have troubles of our own in NATO,' said the American.

'Not Albanian troubles. If you really want to know about troubles in an alliance, try the Albanians for a month.'

# CHAPTER SEVENTEEN

# A BALANCE OF TERROR, A CRISIS OF CONFIDENCE

Europe has been at peace since 1945. This is due, in the view of its supporters, to NATO. They believe that its existence has deterred the Soviet Union from the political adventurism resumed by Stalin as soon as the Second World War ended – the incipient attempts to intimidate independent neighbours like Norway and Denmark as once Hitler intimidated Austria and Czechoslovakia. It is a fact that Stalin drew back from this behaviour in Europe from the moment the Atlantic Alliance was formed.

The opposite view is that there would have been peace without NATO because there was neither a will nor a reason for war in Europe. If anything, the political aims and military presence stemming from the Atlantic Treaty have endangered peace by obliging Russia, made anxious by NATO rhetoric and collective strength, to maintain a high level of armaments to defend itself and its allies. Implicit in this contention is the belief that the Soviet Union has never posed a threat to the European or North American democracies.

A third view, evolving since the 1960s, is that the two superpowers have pulled their allies into respective armed camps to support a particular brand of national power politics, the one to secure America's supremacy as the world's policeman and manager of commerce under the banner of capitalism, the other to establish Russia's international dominance under the red flag. Each is as guilty of warmongering as the other; there is nothing to choose between them. If the invasion of Afghanistan is cited as evidence that Russia is ready to use military force beyond settled frontiers when the political risk is low, the rejoinder is American intervention in Vietnam or its support for counter-revolutionaries in small states such as Nicaragua. Who, then, is the political aggressor, the opportunist, the bully?

In attempting to judge the validity of these latter views, the perspective of history may be helpful. Whatever the merits or demerits of United States policy and practice in Vietnam, or in backing groups such as the Contras in central America, its record as a democratic state cannot seriously be in question. American withdrawal from Vietnam, for example, was due to public disenchantment with the nation's involvement. Meetings were freely called to express public opposition to government policy. Their proceedings and the views of others were regularly reported, together with many other criticisms of government policy in a free press. Public influence was, and is, able to be exerted in national elections by secret ballot for the Congress every two years. The Congress is independent of the government, the judiciary independent of both. The United States has no political prisoners. Its citizens are free to travel in and out of their country and to listen to the broadcasts of foreign radio stations without let or hindrance. Occasional attempts in various administrations to carry through secretly ventures at odds with the law have invariably been exposed, often with disastrous consequences for the perpetrators.

None of these liberties or the benefits which flow from them are available to the people of the Soviet Union. The suggestion that all has changed since the death of Stalin in 1953 ignores the events in Hungary of 1956, or the later interventions in Czechoslovakia and Afghanistan. The imprisonment of political dissidents did not stop when Stalin died.

Those who believe that these perceptions are false or exaggerated could argue that the Soviet Union poses no threat to anyone. Alternatively, accepting them, it might be said that what Russia does internally is its own affair, and that it has a right to defend itself, hence its need of a *cordon sanitaire* of friendly states.

There is another unhappy echo of the past here. Those who sympathised with Hitler responded in much the same way to criticism of his policies and their consequences. Indeed, those who now deny that there is a lack of liberty in Russia or that its rulers threaten peace, employ arguments similar to those used to whitewash Hitler's form of rule and disregard of international obligations in the 1930s, sometimes expressing them in the phraseology of his apologists. What Hitler did internally was indeed his own affair and that of the German people, at any rate those who supported him in millions in the last free election of his regime.

140

Governments and peoples of other nations had the right to criticise Hitler's regime, to aid victims of his cruelty and to restrict diplomatic or commercial relations, but no more, so long as the depravity of the Nazi state was confined to its internal functioning. But just as Hitler had a right, and a duty, as the Soviet leadership has now, to defend the homeland, other states had and have still the same duty when threatened by external aggression, as once by Nazi Germany, so now by the Soviet Union. Hitler's overseas supporters argued that he broke treaties or incorporated other states to bring the German people into one nation, and to offer them the opportunity to prosper. When he extended his activities into the realms of those who were plainly not Germans, it was contended that he needed such territories for the mutual security of his own and the native peoples. On the same lines, myths have been propounded conveniently for the Soviet Union, some of which have gained remarkable credence. It is said that Russia has had so much of its territory taken away by conquest over past centuries that there is national anxiety to prevent a recurrence of these losses. This is a fable. It is similarly convenient for foreign admirers to offer the suggestion that the Soviet Union needs a *cordon sanitaire* of states to assure its security.

Russian adventurism outside the Iron Curtain may have diminished with the death of Stalin but it has not come to an end. The ability to pursue policies of this nature by force of arms has been fully maintained. The state has remained militarised under his successors – Messrs Malenkov, Khrushchev, Brezhnev, Andropov, Chernenko to Gorbachev – by the following criteria.

- It is a totalitarian, single-party state.

- The party not only decides and oversees general strategy, but also purely military strategy, including that at front level, and extends control into tactical levels through political officers, and party place men.

- Prior to conscription for military service, all schoolboys are required to undertake professionally organised military training.

- Quite apart from her Warsaw Pact allies, the Soviet Union maintains a very high number of forces under arms – sixty tank, motorised rifle and airborne divisions at full strength,

141

for example, in eastern Europe and European Russia.* These are backed by huge reserves in men and military equipment and supplies.

- The character of her armed forces – that is, the ships in her fleets, the nature of her field formations, land and air – is aggressive. They are supported by second- and third-line replacement and supply echelons to carry its armies and their forces in Europe, for example, to the Atlantic coast of France. ,

- The training of these forces and the exercises which they regularly undertake are based upon an unvaried theme of offensive action.

- Special formations – *spetsnaz* – have been trained to engage in terrorism inside the European democracies in time of crisis.

The cost of maintaining this policy of militarisation is high and rising, consuming a major share of Russian resources – men and materials – in science and technology. Some indication of this was given in an article by Major-General Professor Gurov in *Krasnya zvezda* in December 1982.

Under present-day conditions the inter-relationship between military matters and the economy has become unusually close, and demands on material provision for troops and naval forces have increased sharply. First, there has been an unprecedented increase in the volume and a substantial alteration in the structure of the military consumption of material facilities and resources. Second, armies and navies are now equipped with the most complex systems of weapons and military hardware, which, furthermore, are virtually renewed every ten to twelve years which requires a highly developed and dynamic economy and advanced scientific and technical potential. Third, there has been an increase in manpower costs and the costs of means of armed struggle. Fourth, substantially greater demands have

---

* The mobilisation potential of the army in the Soviet Union exceeds 200 divisions (tank, motorised rifle and airborne). That of the United States is forty tank, mechanised, airborne and infantry divisions (or divisional equivalents in independent brigades).

been made on the moral-political qualities and general educational, technical and professional training both of workers
engaged in the military production sphere and armed forces
personnel.

When this was written, the Red Army was engaged in an
armaments programme which *inter alia* enlarged the weaponry of its
field·force divisions in Europe by almost a third, including the
entry of 2,300 new main battle tanks a year amongst its overall
number of 52,600. It was also constructing a series of new 65,000-
ton aircraft carriers.

Such programmes are indeed expensive. Because the government
of the Soviet Union does not lay its gigantic military budgets before
a critical legislature for scrutiny and challenge, the full extent of the
charge on state resources is obscured. Details of defence expenditure published in Moscow from time to time are false: the sums
shown are inadequate to provide for the manifest defence forces. It
is generally accepted that actual outlay is much higher – whatever
the sum. Russian apologists and others, for example in 'peace
movements', still say that this expenditure is simply defensive, a
response to fear of attack by the West.

In any test, this explanation fails. For example, in the desolate
tundra of the Kola peninsula, running north of Leningrad to the
Arctic Ocean, the Red Army has completed in the past ten years the
construction of nineteen first-class airfields with runways capable of
operating all classes of military aircraft, and equipped with
installations for a full range of distant and close ground-to-air
defences, underground fuel bunkers, armaments stores and the
most modern base aids for all-weather operations, including
fighter-direction facilities. It is also developing further the extensive naval base in and around Murmansk and uprating the six
motorised rifle divisions and the airborne division in the region.
But against whom? The scant numbers of the neighbouring Finnish
defence forces, in no way involved in NATO, scarcely threaten
Russian territory. Neither do those of Norway, with a population of
little more than four million and a single standing brigade in its
field forces, most of which are engaged in their civil occupations
hundreds of miles distant from the Russo-Norwegian border.
Though allies come to train in the country, Norway does not permit
the basing of foreign NATO units in its territory in peacetime.

For its part, Norway is acutely conscious of the fact that, due to geography, its airfields in Troms could be used to inhibit the passage to and from the Atlantic of the Grand Northern Fleet of the Soviet Navy in war. These provide the focus for the seven Russian divisions in the Kola and a naval amphibious force which includes additional armour and infantry, together with the strategic and tactical air forces regularly exercised from the air bases facing the frontiers of Finland and Norway. Norway feels threatened because the Soviet Union maintains and exercises a potential for the capture of her northern provinces.

In the same region, the aggressive nature of the Soviet Northern Fleet, based in Murmansk, is manifest. It includes one, sometimes two, aircraft carriers together with eighty other principal warships including cruisers, destroyers and frigates. This is an ocean-going battle fleet far in excess of Russian needs to defend its interests in the Barents Sea which are, in any case, well within the striking radii of the Kola airfields. Aside from the forty submarines in the fleet carrying nuclear missiles, there are also 138 maritime attack submarines. Russia enjoys the advantage of interior lines of communication and supply and its territory is largely protected by a cordon of allied states in Europe. With a limited sea frontage in the West, the deployment of a submarine force in its Northern Fleet greater in strength than that of the entire German Navy in 1940 must be regarded as offensive in intention.*

NATO has neither the political character not the military means of launching an attack against Russia or into the territory of its Warsaw Pact allies. Whilst the supreme allied commanders have the authority to take preliminary defensive measures if the strategic threat is heightened by the Soviet Union, these do not extend to the initiation of hostilities. As noted, there are no plans for such contingencies. The Atlantic Treaty embodies a political and a defence committee but these are not supra-national authorities to mobilise reservists, despatch reinforcing units from home bases, and break out war stocks in a crisis. Such measures can only be authorised by individual member governments and would be taken only as the result of a military onslaught or strong indications that

* Germany had 99 submarines in service for operations throughout the world in 1940. In addition to the Russian submarines in the Northern Fleet, there are a further 152 hunter/killer or attack submarines in other fleets.

an attack was imminent. The armed forces allocated by each government to NATO, whether out of or already in the NATO regions, have formally to be passed by the head of government or other minister to the particular NATO commander nominated to receive and operate them. Until that transfer of authority has been made, the national commanders and their subordinates concerned are unable, as a matter of the law of their particular country, to accept a NATO commander's orders.

It is sometimes suggested that the United States, impatient with or disdaining the reluctance of its allies to engage in war, might attack Russia alone. The idea is absurd. America depends upon the European allies for its entry ports, roads, railways and operating bases. If these were denied them by political interdict, they would be powerless to engage in hostilities. In any case, the United States Army has only two corps permanently in Germany. Its component in the tactical air forces there, if operating alone, would be attacking into a Warsaw Pact strength seven times its size. Its ground-to-air defence chain would be fragmentary.

Though of a lower order, the West's military weakness persists even when all NATO forces are mobilised and first-line war stocks opened. This does not stem simply from the circumstance of being considerably outnumbered on land and in the air, though the numbers of trained reserves available to the NATO forces are clearly insufficient to sustain the demands of conventional war for more than a few weeks. A second notable constraint upon operating options is the inadequacy of the support train to carry forward the land and air forces in an offensive of any sort, or to permit a prolonged defence. Unlike the comprehensive transport and supply echelons of the Red Army, most of the national armed forces in NATO lack a third line, some even a complete second line, essential to the maintenance of an advancing armed host consuming the extraordinary quantities of fuel, ammunition, replacement assemblies and spare parts for sustained offensive action. The situation of the Allied forces rolling forward towards the Low Countries and Germany in the late summer of 1944, when a temporary crisis in transportation almost brought the advance to a halt, illustrates the dependence of an army's teeth upon its administrative tail, a dependence which grows greater as technology advances. With the exception of the United States and, to an extent, of Britain, France, and the Federal Republic of Germany, none of the NATO countries has the home manufacturing capacity to refill third- or second-line stocks of war materials for defence as these are consumed in the first line. Though the United States manufacturing base would be capable of providing a continuous resupply for the defensive needs of her own armed forces, it would not, without considerable time to reorganise its industries, have the capacity to supply others. Even so, her own supplies would have to be carried by sea and air over a considerable distance to the European theatre, while the factories of the United Kingdom, France and Germany would be subject to damage, perhaps destruction, by conventional air attack.

NATO's relative military weakness in conventional arms and support is precisely the reason why it has maintained and developed a range of nuclear weapons, from the nuclear 155 mm shell to strategic intercontinental ballistic missiles. In Europe, the NATO supreme allied commander is painfully aware that, in the event of war, because his reinforcements and supplies are so few, his front would quickly be broken open at one or more critical points. Every commander from army battalion and air squadron upwards knows that, however valiantly his unit fights, casualties and the consumption of ammunition and equipment at battle rates of intensity rapidly exhaust the reserves available. Assuming that the NATO member states will not significantly increase the burden of expense of their level of forces, NATO strategy will continue to be inextricably interconnected with nuclear weapons in the face of Warsaw Pact strength in conventional forces.

Nuclear operations, limitation and control have almost become an esoteric subject. Seek to identify some simple reference points to aid comprehension and they will be speedily split into an infinite number by the experts who thrive on the subtle inferences and implications of treaty drafts, the sophistry of multiple independently targetable re-entry vehicles and the defensive – and offensive – options of 'star wars'. From the Russian side, philosophy and data will be further obscured by propaganda clouds spread to disguise the intensity with which the Soviet nuclear industry is working on the same projects they condemn in America. Even so, the attempt must be made to identify salient points.

First, a fragment of the numbers stocked would, if detonated, be sufficient to destroy the human race; multilateral and unilateral disarmers agree on that, if nothing else, when they argue ways and means of disposing of such weapons of mass destruction. Latterly, these discussions seem to overlook the fact that the capability to eradicate mankind has been with us for several decades. The Cuban crisis reminded participants and onlookers, if a reminder was needed, that in nuclear war government and people would find themselves on the battlefield. Air raids by bombers and rockets in the Second World War had already suggested the vulnerability of the interiors of homelands to many in Europe and the Far East. Refinements such as multiple warheads, each with a guidance system able to direct it on to an individual target, simply increase the rate of devastation, making the prospect of a pyrrhic victory more likely.

The possession by the two alliances of a roughly equal number of nuclear weapons was described a generation ago as providing 'a balance of terror'. The notion that possession of such power would lead inevitably to its being used, an assertion made often in the debates of the 1960s when nuclear weapons control and disarmament philosophy was developing, is now rarely expressed. Time and circumstances have not tended to support this doom-laden prophecy. Still, the terror persists. Some are acutely conscious of it. Few are immune from an uneasy apprehension of its presence in the background. But the power which terrifies us remains leashed because parity has been maintained. Whatever is done to reduce the risks of being engulfed by nuclear attack requires that the balance continues at all stages of reduction. Those who advocate unilateral nuclear disarmament might consider that they are using the same arguments as those who urged a reduction in armaments in the 1930s, including the much-feared bomber aircraft. They hoped this would persuade Hitler to do the same. While much of Europe and both states of North America disarmed, Germany – and Japan – rearmed.

A curious feature of the arguments of many nuclear unilateralists is that, in removing the nuclear weights from one side of the scales, the danger of war may be averted by replacing them with conventional forces. The rationale is that the Warsaw Pact is strong in this field where NATO is weak: strengthen the latter and there will be stalemate. But has the behaviour of the Soviet Union's leadership at any point during the past seventy years been such as to convince those whom it confronts that it will not exploit sole possession of nuclear weapons as Hitler exploited the superiority of the *Wehrmacht*?

Parity in nuclear weapons has made for stability. Mankind may have been walking through the valley of the shadow of death since mutually opposing camps deployed the atom bomb, but the track through it has so far proved secure enough. As far as anyone can see, it appears to run on, affording a passage through the dangers that threaten. This is no time to start stumbling off into the darkness to seek a smoother track. It is far from sure that there is one.

# CHAPTER EIGHTEEN

# SCENARIOS FOR WAR

As the world enters each cycle of disarmament negotiations, newspapers and magazines, radio and television programmes, in America and Europe engage experts and commentators to suggest what the outcome will be. Editors seem ever ready to give space and time to prophets even though, judging by past performance, most are likely to prove false. But if past experience has scarcely instructed those in the news and current affairs industry, it has taught a few lessons to governments of the Atlantic Alliance, principally the United States, despite the distractions of party considerations. High-level negotiations in foreign policy have matured somewhat since the American secretary of state, Jimmy Byrnes, sat in the Spiridonevka Palace in Moscow with Bevin and Molotov in the winter of 1945, 'playing his negotiations by ear', in the view of George Kennan, minister at the United States embassy. 'In the present conference, his weakness in dealing with the Russians is that his main purpose is to achieve some sort of agreement, he doesn't much care what.' Since then, Dr Kissinger has demonstrated the merits of leverage.

Meanwhile, the NATO military advisers sit on the touchline like coaches at a game who are apprehensive that their players may get carried away by the clamour of the crowd and ignore their signals. If they press advice too robustly upon their team of politicians they will be reminded that 'War is too serious a matter to be left to the generals.' Some of the admirals, generals and air marshals may feel tempted to reply that politics is too serious a matter to be left to the politicians, the disarmament field being no exception. Perhaps their best course might be simply to display a text on the desks of their principals each morning; say, Bishop Butler's observation: 'Things and actions are what they are, and the consequences of them will be what they will be: why then should we desire to be deceived?'

If there is to be disarmament, the hope of the national and NATO commanders is that it will be staged and balanced, leaving them throughout the process with the wherewithal to conduct operations if the political climate should suddenly change. From the time that NATO forces began to form as an entity, through disarmament negotiations relating to nuclear weapons, conventional force levels and chemical weapons, fear of an attack with strategic and tactical surprise upon their territories has lain upon its principal commanders. Overt and covert intelligence has confirmed consistently that Russia has that military capability in Europe and suggested a political readiness for war on the part of the Soviet government if it offered ample prospects of success. On their side, the anxieties of the NATO military chiefs have been recurrently stirred by reflection on the weakness of their own operating circumstances and resources.

Thus the apprehension persists of a summer's day, as it might be, when the maximum number of those permitted to be on leave are away from their duties in the common NATO defence. Conventional air raids begin upon their bases and troop locations as the tank and motorised rifle divisions of the Warsaw Pact forces cross the frontier under covering fire from artillery and rockets; parachutists and helicopter-borne infantry descend; and marines storm ashore from the Barents, Baltic and Black Seas. There may have been a few days of warning. The calling out of reserves coinciding with movements on land, at sea, and in the activation of forward airfields may have indicated, perhaps, deployment of the Warsaw Pact for war. These signs may have been made more ominous by reliable reports that fuel and ammunition have been issued from depots in East Germany, Poland, Byelorussia and Carpathia. At best, the NATO member governments may have been sufficiently alarmed to begin mobilisation. At worst, as the offensive opens, all are still debating what their reaction to these indications of danger should be while fleeting opportunities to order mobilisation and to deploy the standing forces are lost as war begins.

In the Federal Republic of Germany, the movement forward of troops to the frontiers is difficult because they are frequently attacked from the air and impeded by hordes of refugees rushing to distance themselves from the battle zone. The main body of enemy divisions close up to those of the hastily gathered arrays of the standing forces of the Federal German Army and the Dutch, British, Belgian and American corps with whom they will fight. The enemy begins with a double superiority in strength: in overall numbers and in concentrations at chosen points of thrust. The defenders, uncertain of where the latter are at the outset, are obliged to cover the front on the Barents Sea, in the Baltic approaches, from the Elbe to the Czech and Austrian borders, against excursions from Bulgaria, or across the north-east border of Turkey with Russia. At sea, the Soviet fleets are out and submarines are launching their torpedoes as the air and land attacks begin.

Take a single point of thrust on the Central Front in Germany. Towards selected points of encounter, the Russian forces travel forward in column, tanks one behind the other, under the protection of strong air defences. NATO air and ground obser- vation units, combining with electronic intelligence, warn that a Soviet division is approaching an area defended by one or two battle groups, roughly, nine battalions attacking two. Preceded by air strikes and artillery fire, closing to engagement range, they move out on either side of their axis. Tank guns open fire at, say, 3,500 yards from their targets, anti-tank guided missiles and rockets at lesser ranges. Accepting the delays of tactical movement across country, the enemy vehicles, tanks and infantry in armoured carriers on tracks or wheels, will be among the NATO forces in about thirty minutes from that first engagement. This is the period in which the defence has to destroy the greater part of the attacking force or choose one of two options: to be overwhelmed or to withdraw. Where the attacker is four times the strength of the defender such rapid destruction or immobilisation by the latter would be extraordinary.

The defence is not firing at static targets. It is itself under fire from the air, from artillery, and from troops moving forward against it. There is the interplay of the advancing armoured infantry, infiltrating into the cover from which the defending tanks are firing, and the counter-operations of the defending infantry. Assume that the defence has chosen its ground cunningly, uses its weapons skilfully and enjoys continuous support from its own artillery and intermittently from the air to the point that it has

151

reduced the attack advantage to about two to one. It then engages in a close-quarters battle in which craft and luck combine to destroy or eject the remnant of the attack.

When the first brief moments of relief and elation have passed among those who have stood or recovered their ground, when heartbeats are moderating and a strife-free breath has been taken, the tally of losses among the defence – men, weapons, equipment and supply – is collated. It will not be negligible. It is a diminished defence, therefore, that has to deal with the next attack, and the next, and the next. Though the enemy are not supermen, are delayed by the problems of obtaining information as to losses and shifting defence locations prior to mounting the next attack, their weight on the ground and in the air, and the depth of their resources, will day by day break the limited resources of those who oppose them. The flow of trained reinforcements to the defence will dry up. Their resupply of ammunition, tank shot, guided missiles, artillery shells and mortar bombs will diminish. The slender reserves of the smaller NATO nations will be exhausted. At one or more points, a breach will be made: the defence will either be destroyed where it stands or swept aside. The divisional reserve or the army reserve or the front exploitation force of the Warsaw Pact will pass through into relatively open country. After such days of intense struggle, the reserves of the NATO corps commanders and, behind them, the army group commanders, will be scant. Scraping all their resources, land and air together, they may be able to stem one or two important breaches in their forward areas but will then lack the means to contain others.

Behind the first echelon of the Warsaw Pact offensive comes a second, equally strong. The only second echelon available to NATO, and that by negotiation, is the field army of France. But unless the French government decides to hold it back until a victorious foe arrives on its frontiers, it will have been committed to the initial battles in southern Germany. Its air squadrons will have joined with the allied tactical air forces striving to knock out the enemy airfields and the aircraft using them; to engage in interdiction of the forward land battle; to answer as often as possible the calls of the land forces to get the enemy air forces off their backs and to participate in the struggle among the forward defended localities. Everywhere they will be at a considerable disadvantage in numbers but the penalty will be felt most by those striking into enemy territory. The numbers of Warsaw Pact air-defence fighters opposing the NATO raiders will correspond to the relative strengths on the ground: four to one.

At sea, the Warsaw Pact submarines, principally Russian, engage in considerable destruction of ships bringing men and war supplies across the Atlantic to the NATO commands in northern, central and southern Europe. The NATO Atlantic Fleet is engaged in preventing the break-in of the reinforced Russian Northern Fleet to the Atlantic. Loss of the NATO Atlantic Fleet would lead to the loss of sea lanes for merchant ships. The early capture of Iceland by a Red Army force would shift the balance of this critical operation in Russia's favour. If the northern Norwegian airfields have been lost, the Russians will enjoy a considerable advantage in maritime air striking power. If Denmark has been lost, the Baltic approaches will have passed into Soviet control; maritime considerations aside, there will be no air defences between Russian aircraft operating from captured Danish airfields and the United Kingdom's shores.

Such a scenario persuaded a Danish politician to suggest that, in the first hour of an offensive by the Warsaw Pact, a brief recorded message should automatically be sent by the Western allies to Moscow: 'We surrender'. We surrender because, after a week or ten days of conventional battles, the supreme allied commander in Europe would be obliged to tell the heads of NATO governments that the only way in which he could continue the struggle with any hope of stabilising it would involve the use of nuclear weapons. In the view of that Dane, such a course could not be adopted.

The scenario is no longer wholly valid, however. The circumstances of battle described obtained for the first twenty-five years of NATO's existence, but a number of factors, political and military, have changed. So has the technology of war.

Technology has helped to lessen the imbalance between the two sides as the following instances, by no means exhaustive, indicate. First, the danger of being surprised has been reduced by the inception of observation satellites complemented by the electronic gadgetry carried in high-flying jet aircraft, the NATO airborne early-warning system. Together they have made the spy in the woods, the agent lurking behind the window, redundant as a means of spotting the passing of armies, ships and aircraft into battle array, or the deployment of mobile nuclear launchers.

Rocketry and guidance systems have also transformed what used to be called anti-aircraft defence. 'Ack-ack' as the Engish had it in two world wars was a very coarse art, more a bugaboo than a bolt. It was incapable of defending, for example, the *Prince of Wales* and *Repulse* off the coast of Malaya in 1941. Now the air-defence rockets reach up to 60,000 feet to home on their aerial targets. Many air-defence missiles have the intelligence to ignore the deliberately misleading signals directed at them by the enemy's counter-electronic measures. Some of these weapons have been miniaturised to permit the launching of a missile from a tube on a soldier's shoulder which has a high chance of destroying a low-flying aircraft ten thousand times more expensive than itself, disregarding the inestimable value of the pilot's life. Low-fliers are also hazarded by multiple cannon and machine-guns aligned against them by guidance systems.

The NATO air-defence crews on the ground expect to destroy any enemy aircraft which penetrate their defence zones within their radii of engagement, given a continuous supply of missiles – which may be in question. The high standard of their handling skills, in combination with a comprehensive warning and fire-co-ordination system, validate their confidence. Friendly fighter interceptors would only inhibit their roles. In any case, the complexity and expense of modern aircraft, and the time that it takes to train aircrew, indicate that they should be removed from the hazard of their fire at the lower and medium levels to those above, say, in excess of 50,000 feet. But this is not the sphere of the 'dogfight'. Flying an aircraft at the very high speeds in all weather, and at night, the pilot will be expecting to pick up intruders far beyond optical range. He will triumph by monitoring a continuing flow of varied information on which, selectively, he may act after a few seconds of judgement. In that high vault, co-operation with the NATO airborne early-warning aircraft and his own ground support in electronic warfare will help him to cope with superior numbers. As on the ground, the abiding problem is to overcome superior numbers.

The hazards of the enemy ground-based air defences will fall to comrades flying interdiction and strike missions. Along their routes will lie the matured expertise of the Warsaw Pact air-defence systems. Their chances of success in applying their weapons and returning safely will be enhanced by technology to assist in flying close to the nap of the earth below the defensive radars, in electronic counter-measures to deny periodic exposure to the enemy's missiles and cannon.

On the battlefield below, the tank has been modernised, its armour toughened, its mobility increased, the power and accuracy of its main armament, the direct-fire gun, enhanced. It has, however, become very heavy in consequence – in excess of sixty tons fully laden – and although further developments will reduce weight, numbers of crew and size of gun, it is becoming increasingly vulnerable to attack. The decisive weapon platform on the open battlefield for more than sixty years, the tank in its present form has peaked and, though it is too painful for many of its operators to recognise yet, is declining in value. But its day is not yet done: it is still the only land weapon which combines a capacity for offence and defence. Battles may be contained but they will not be won by the new range of anti-tank weapons.

Even so, the latter make an important contribution to the defensive battle. Artillery munitions have been developed to rain intelligent bomblets precisely on the top sides of armoured vehicles. The infantry now have numerous portable guided missiles which can engage tanks or armoured personnel carriers up to 2,000 metres distant. They can be fired from concealed positions which will not often be betrayed by the light noise or the small plume of smoke on discharge among the turbulence of the contact zone. Frontal, turret and some side armour on tanks will rarely be penetrated by the warheads of these missiles, but if they do nothing else but break the tracks or jam the turret-ring they will have repaid their purchase many times over. The destruction of armoured personnel carriers and others in that family, well within their capability, will also pay a high dividend. Possession of such portable weapons permits brigade commanders in defence to draw in the greater number of their tanks, many of which, formerly, were of necessity deployed as mobile anti-tank guns. A tank reserve of consequence can thereby be created for local counter-offensive action.

Larger anti-tank guided weapons, matching the effective range of tanks, have also now entered the NATO armouries. These are most efficiently carried on the helicopter. Ignorance and prejudice have combined, notoriously among the British services, to delay the extraordinary value of this rapid response to armoured thrusts threatening to break through a crumbling defence. The very fast, light attack helicopters are able to bring their fire power to bear long before land reserves based at the same distance. The larger transport helicopters have the capacity to bring forward quickly infantry with portable anti-tank missiles to seal a breach, carrying also light vehicles to give the teams essential local mobility. Helicopters are less vulnerable to fire than was at first expected. Their value in other duties – reconnaissance, liaison, casualty evacuation, movement of artillery or engineer stores, and resupply – has made them indispensable to a successful defensive action.

Common among these and many other technological marvels is the great leap forward in facilities for what the military call 'C3': command, control and communications. The days when naval, land and air signal officers retained a vocabulary of excuses for not establishing radio contact – 'skip distance, sir', 'there is an electric storm over the Sargasso Sea', 'the other end is not responding' – are over. There are now so many channels, many impervious to enemy eavesdroppers, that they are used to excess – but correction of that is a matter of discipline. Magic boxes sort messages automatically. Information on every subject may be displayed graphically at the touch of a button. Contractors seek to interest commanders-in-chief in knowing every detail of their command to the number of pencils in every supply depot. The exploitation of such facilities, balanced by discretion in the information displayed, will take time, but their inception has provided NATO with the means to make best use of scarce resources, to avoid the loss of detachments isolated at a distance and to deceive the attacking enemy.

The establishment of permanent headquarters for the supreme allied commander in Europe and his three regional commanders-in-chief almost forty years ago was an important contribution to deterrence. But the value lay then more in the manifestation of alliance than the level of military effectiveness. Accession of numbers and modernisation of forces substantiated narrowly the credibility of the NATO defences. Since then western technology has underpinned it despite Soviet nuclear and conventional expansion.

Throughout each day, every day of the year, the international commanders and staffs maintain their watch and readiness to implement defence plans in partnership with those in national headquarters if the contingency should arise. The NATO Northern Army Group commander no longer expects his ADC to have a pocket full of change for the public telephone boxes.

# CHAPTER NINETEEN

# GLIMPSES OF PEACE

With the passing of the old guard of the Soviet Communist Party, this judgement if no other may be passed upon their works: the objectives of those who carried forward the October Revolution of 1917 have not been achieved. Lenin's expectations of the evolution of a state superior to all others by the application of scientific Socialism, and the concomitant overthrow, from this base, of world capitalism, have not been realised. To the surprise and exasperation of its architects, the construction of a huge apparatus of central power has not only failed in its declared purpose but it has also failed to educate sufficiently the hearts and minds it was designed to control to resist notions alien to Marxism-Leninism.

With each succession in the leadership following Stalin's death, popular reaction inside Russia and its satellites, so far as it has been possible to comprehend it, seems to have been of hope and anxiety mingled. Each new man has prompted among the democracies speculation as to his potential and will for a reduction in the inhumanity of the Kremlin regime towards its subjects, in its abiding hostility – notwithstanding a periodic face of sweet reason – to those abroad who do not court Soviet power.

Hopes of better things were not dashed when Malenkov and his associates murdered Beria, head of the secret police, immediately after Stalin's death; Beria had been the ready agent of the latter and intended to take his master's place, using the tools of their association: terror, intrigue and murder. There was a mood of optimism when Khrushchev not only exposed some of the crimes of Stalin's rule but also permitted Malenkov, whom he deposed, to retire with a pension. The Department of Pensions in Moscow had not previously been much called upon to make payments on this account to high officials and ministers. Hitherto, as it suited the party leader, they had either been killed in office or kept in harness until a natural death released them. Khrushchev benefited similarly when ousted by Brezhnev, who tightened the reigns of power over the next eighteen years. Bureaucracy and repression flourished. Prospects for peace appeared to rise but then fell away. It was a period in which educational and, in relative terms, living standards soared throughout the Soviet Socialist Republics, during which the cult of the leader was refloated and Brezhnev appropriated a second string: the office of president. As head of state, his face became known to the American people as the man who kissed President Carter at the signing of the SALT 2 Treaty. When Brezhnev died his office as party leader was filled briefly by Andropov, a former chief of the KGB – the State Security and Political Intelligence Department – and, on his demise, it passed to a moribund party grandee, Chernenko.

It is interesting that, with each change from Stalin onwards, numerous Western prolocutors and commentators have tended to suggest that more pacific, more humanitarian policies may be expected from the new leader. Various reasons are offered to support the view: the personality of the successor; his distance due to age or other circumstance from the misdeeds of the old Bolsheviks; his pragmatism; his genuine desire for reform; his sure power base within the party, or his lack of it. A corollary has been the condemnation of the errors and evils of the predecessor, often by individuals who had once denied his vices. Confidence is expressed that the newcomer will surely, by his very illumination of these malpractices, eschew them.

Yet disquieting events have continued as one leader has succeeded another. Internally, state persecution has remained the response to political dissidence, with the disposal of persistent offenders to psychiatric wards or remote prison camps in conditions akin to the *Nacht und Nebel* policy in Nazi Germany. Declarations concerning war potential have continued to be false or misleading: notifications of troop reductions in central Europe were more than offset by unannounced increases in the size and strength of formations remaining on the ground; lies and evasions pervaded statements about the development of anti-ballistic missile systems and, on the frontiers of technology, such devices as satellite attack weapons and the Russian form of Star Wars at the very time that Soviet politicians were castigating the American exploration of these options. Attacks were made similarly on the United States proposals to modernise its stock of ageing chemical weapons whilst the Soviet Union was continuing the manufacture of its own advanced forms. There were renewals of propaganda campaigns: the Soviet attempts in 1982–3 to rouse NATO's public opinion in Europe against the fielding of Pershing and cruise missiles while denying the fact that greater numbers of Soviet tactical missiles were being deployed in the same region, a lie exposed by satellite photography; or the prolonged campaign to secure a Nordic nuclear-free zone which was to exclude the Kola peninsula. In the 'peace offensives', there were official denials in Moscow that Soviet money was involved in the campaigns abroad, but the second secretary in the Russian embassy in Copenhagen, Merkulov, was caught red-handed passing funds to a Danish self-styled 'peace activist'. This matter was exposed in the Scandinavian press shortly after a Russian submarine had been caught spying in Swedish waters. There was also the invasion of Afghanistan and the continued denial of human rights inside the Soviet Union, contrary to the agreements made at Helsinki.

Still, all these might be attributed to the errors and omissions to be expected as the old guard moved on. Leonid Brezhnev was born in 1906. He was thus eighteen when Stalin, cutting out his rivals, succeeded the dying Lenin. He rose to power in Stalin's shadow. Mikhail Gorbachev, general secretary of the Soviet Communist Party since 1985, was born in 1931. He may have been reared under the system over which Stalin presided but he owes no special debt of preferment to that personality. He has made an excellent impression by his condemnation of past mistakes – including the abuses of power by officialdom – his reminders that financial and political corruption are incompatible with Socialist morality, and his insistence on the proper application of the law. But some of his predecessors also did this on assuming office. The release of more political prisoners and the granting of a greater number of exit permits to Jews wishing to emigrate to Israel have encouraged hopes at home and abroad that he might be a man of his word. So, too, has the change in news reporting, a function absolutely under party control, whereby there is periodic, timely exposure of events unflattering to party or state. And however superficial they may be as a criterion, Gorbachev's frank appearance, his wife's dress sense and good looks, are reassuring. They seem a civilised pair, not at all the sort of people who would perpetuate the brutalities of the past. Their style is consonant with the new watch words, *glasnost* and *peristroika*, 'openness' and 'reconstruction'.

On this basis, the world outside the Iron Curtain is hoping for a change in policies for the better from the Soviet Union, none more so than the peoples of the democracies. They would be content with the following, suggested to Malenkov by a former British prime minister, Clement Attlee, in 1954.

1. Give the Russian people more freedom.
2. Ease restrictions on the satellite states.
3. Stop trying to undermine other governments.
4. Reduce Soviet armaments – if a general reduction is desirable, it would be a good thing if Russia, the most heavily armed country, set an example.

It would be informative to sit in while the *Politburo*, or its principals, discussed future policy towards the members of the Atlantic Alliance. Presumably some apprehensions have long been relieved. The Federal Republic of Germany, for example, has not emerged as a military state dedicated to aggression. It is manifestly a model of democracy, its armed forces scrupulously regulated. The success of its economy endorses its interest in the preservation of peace. The KGB, two million strong, of whom several hundred thousand are actively engaged in espionage, has long since provided sufficient information to confirm that NATO's armed forces do not have the capacity to mount, still less sustain, an offensive strategy with conventional arms, and that they are marginally behind the offensive potential of the Soviet Union in nuclear capability. There should surely be some recognition among the policy-makers that if the United States should attempt of its own initiative to use its nuclear bases in Europe in aggression against the Soviet Union, these would immediately be taken over by the host governments, if necessary by force. Equally, there should be recognition that the American people, like the western Europeans, are not of a character to support aggression and that the support of a majority would be necessary for war.

A persistent matter of anxiety in the *Politburo*'s discussions on future external policy may be the inability of the Soviet Union to match the Western democracies in the application of science and technology. Russia has more graduate engineers than Japan with a far greater spread of raw materials and ample manpower, yet it lacks the ability to produce in relative terms anything like the industrial wealth of Japan. It has more graduate agronomists than the whole of North America, yet almost every year since the October Revolution agriculture has failed to meet its targets due to 'unseasonable weather'. Once, Nikita Khrushchev declared a timetable during which the Soviet Union would overtake the nations of the West in wealth and prosperity. In these spheres, Russia continues to remain behind.

Without meaning it to do so, Khrushchev's boast was an important signal of hope to those he regarded as his enemies in the West. He was not simply expressing a yearning of his own but of all his countrymen, in that vast land of European and Asiatic peoples, for material improvements in their lives; none more so than those on the inside track, members of the party hierarchy, the *nomenklatura*. Western observers should not assume that all its members are hypocrites or cynics. These men and women have been educated in a closed world dedicated to the realisation of Communism, which has steeped the minds of the receptive in its glories and irrevocability. They long to demonstrate that their system can match and ultimately surpass, the capacity of capitalism for wealth creation and distribution and they want to see it happening in their lifetime. And quite apart from the aspirations of the political zealots, there is the stimulus of national pride. The Russians are no less patriotic than other peoples, rather more so than some. They want to show that they are at least the equals, if not the superiors, of other nations.

This deeply felt wish is denied pre-eminently by the cost of maintaining a huge military establishment. It engages a great number of advanced scientists and technologists, occupies vast manufacturing resources, workers, plant and materials, and consumes huge quantities of the national revenues without productive benefit to the state. The rising burden debilitates the economy.

All this, pacifists may cry gleefully, could be said of the member states of NATO. It is not true. NATO's resources are greater, yet a smaller proportion is allocated to defence. Precisely because its governments, left or right of centre, believe that they must limit their expenditure on defence, NATO's conventional forces are inferior in number and in depth of support to those of the Soviet Union. Hence NATO's dependence on nuclear weapons for the deterrence of war.

Without in any way abandoning its duty to defend its frontiers robustly, Russia has therefore the option to improve its economy by selective measures of disarmament. Simply by running down its overwhelmingly offensive potential, a considerable saving would be effected. Whether they have looked at their armaments policy in precisely that way or not, the need to contain expenditure is apparent to state and party. However, there are other important factors militating for reductions in and modifications to a defensive strategy: manpower, and changes in the nature of Soviet and Soviet satellite man.

The birth rate in European Russia is declining and consequently so are the numbers of men whose first language is Russian. Officially, race makes no difference within the state but as it is policy not to have complete regiments manned by the peoples among whom they are stationed but to have multi-racial units, there are practical difficulties in the instruction of soldiers who are not Slavs, and problems of social isolation of individuals from racial minorities. As this trend is continuing, the Red Army could in due course be manned largely by men from those minorities. It is not a prospect relished by the hierarchy of the armed forces or the *Politburo*. National tradition is still a factor of influence in such matters. The Russian empire, royal or revolutionary, has been run principally by European Russians. A reduction in the numbers required for military service would mitigate the difficulty.*

In theory, the conscript arriving at a barracks or post to begin his two or three years of full-time military service† will be morally, intellectually and, to an extent, professionally attuned to make the best of the period. From infancy, he will have been reminded of the heroic duty of the Red Army to defend his country. Remembrance of those who died in the Second World War – 'the Great Patriotic War' – is celebrated by the state on a particular day of the year but

---

* Not all fit young men are conscripted because there are insufficient places for them. Those not called tend to be in the lower educational and skill categories; or young men with a notably bad record of behaviour. Some in higher education serve only for a year in reserve officer schools.
† Broadly, two years in the land and air forces, three in the navy.

it is also a feature of many other national or local events. Party and government frequently call out the veterans with their medals to honour them. It is a method of political education. In a selection of books for children learning to read are titles such as *A Soldier Was Walking Along the Street*', a simple history of the Red Army since the October Revolution. At seven, children are encouraged to join the 'Octobrists', at ten the 'Pioneers'. The rules of the latter remind members that 'A pioneer reveres the memory of fallen fighters and prepares to become a defender of the Motherland.' There is further education in the history of the Red Army at Pioneer gatherings and elementary military and civil-defence training, particularly at the summer camps. Those who join the Young Communist League at fifteen will continue this training in and out of camp. Some young people join DOSAAF, the Voluntary Society for Co-operation with the Army, Air Force and Navy – rather more than a cadet force as it provides beginners' courses in military specialisations.

The voluntary movements have been active since the 1930s but they have never retained a majority of young people. When the Law of Universal Military Service reduced the terms in 1967 from four and three to the present three and two years, military training prior to conscription became compulsory. Boys and girls – though girls are not conscripted – are committed to a programme (NVP) of seventy hours of classroom and practical work in each of the last two years of education, which extends equally to those youths who, having left school at sixteen, are in first employment. At a glance, there is a resemblance in this scheme to the militarisation of youth in Japan during the 1930s: Communism replaces the Shinto ethos; in both the image of the warrior is exalted, his skills are taken up.

In so far as the party's aims for the youth movements and DOSAAF are concerned, the similarity has substance; but as in many areas of Soviet central and local government, grand schemes have failed because the necessary resources are scarce and too many of the officials charged with implementation lack competence and interest. The NVP programme has failed to provide sufficient instructors or firing ranges, aids or even, for youths at work, teaching sites. Twenty years after inception, special measures are still being taken to remedy these shortcomings.

The Communist Party organisation, whose members are expected to be activists wherever they work, seeks to enthuse, or at least to focus the mind of, the recruit in the matter of his responsibilities immediately prior to his departure for military service. Sending-off parties are sometimes organised to this end. More commonly, greetings cards, on public sale, are given to the young man. On the front there might be the coloured emblem of the Red Army or the USSR. Inside there will be a printed message, of which the following is an example:

> Dear Comrade! We heartily congratulate you and your family on a great and important event in your life – enrolment in the ranks of the armed forces of the USSR... Let your inspiration be the hard-won military achievements of the older generation of your countrymen, and the glorious banners of our Motherland and beloved Soviet Army. Do not stint your strength so that your efforts may increase her glory.
>
> We are confident that you will fulfil your military duty with merit and honour. Your family and relations and the collective in which you work or study will be made proud of your success...

These celebrations outdo those of party, family and friends in Nazi Germany despatching the young man called for service in the armed forces reconstituted by Hitler. There, too, he was to 'defend the Fatherland' as a sacred duty, though young men exhorted in this way were soon forcing a way into the fatherland or motherland of others. But if the young German tended to respond with enthusiasm to his call, there is much evidence that the majority of young Russians today are no more or less eager to undertake military service than their peers in democratic society.

Part of this is no doubt due to the fact that many recruits have not been away from home before and are homesick. Then, their terms of service are worse than those of young men serving in north and western Europe in pay, in barrack amenities and in liberty. The young Soviet soldier has no right to go on leave. A fragment of each intake, cited as 'exceptional soldiers', will be granted ten-day passes to go home; the remainder will not see home at all until their colour service is over. A greater number are likely to be permitted short-term passes to spend a few hours in the local town on a Sunday or special holiday; otherwise, the individal conscript is not allowed out of barracks off duty, and may not even go to see a friend in another unit's lines on the same post without specific permission. In any case, his spare time is very limited; he is training six days a week until 18.00. Monday to Saturday he will also be occupied for three hours each evening in political education, technical maintenance and sport.

Like most forces based on recruitment by conscription, the Red Army in peacetime is a huge training organisation. The greater part of this effort is in the basic and specialist training of its youth, its junior leaders – one in five of whom are officers, regular or reserve – and its multitude of technicians. Because of the increasing complexity of weapons and equipment manned by private soldiers, there is a reliance on the improved standards of education of Soviet youth. The standards of technicians, non-commissioned officers and officers need to be higher still. The school system is meeting these demands. But better education, essential to material progress, was also expected to enhance political reliability. However, the political branch of the armed forces has made periodic observations that better schooling has not made young men more, but rather less, ready to accept their duties and responsibilities as soldiers. Particular complaints have related to indiscipline, mostly of a petty nature, but not simply the long-standing offences of drunkenness and 'hooliganism', rather a greater disregard of regulations and, linked to the latter, a want of 'conscience'. For example, men who have been graded as 'exceptional soldiers' and enjoyed a ten-day leave on the strength of it are seen to be less than zealous when they return and that incentive has been exploited. In short, too many conscripts are artful dodgers and smart-alecks, too many are motivated by self-interest rather than socialist competition.

Appeals for a more imaginative and dynamic leadership by regular officers, warrant and senior non-commissioned officers, and for a greater exercise of 'socialist morality' are made to counter these tendencies. The difficulty is to get the generality of leaders, regular and conscript, to exercise their authority, to take the initiative. What the most senior military and political officers apparently fail to see is that the problem is intractable unless changes are made in the way the state operates as a whole. The apolitical armed forces in the Western democracies are sometimes criticised by public and private bodies for maintaining old values and disciplines which are out of kilter with the practice of the nation. Soviet military society reflects precisely the practice of the nation. For example, in exercises, a subordinate commander does not tell his superiors that his battalion, regiment or even division is

165

facing such strength that a moderation or change of plan should be considered. He expects to remain in operations until casualties make his command inoperable. At lower levels, it is not a common practice for the junior leaders to engage in initiatives of their own. No doubt the officer corps has its young Turks and some of these succeed in conducting policy as they choose; but they do not succeed if they act contrary to party policy or expose party errors. Most of their colleagues prefer to keep a low profile. If criticism published in the open journals is an indicator, a strong element of political officers do the same. Time-serving and a clean record bring a sufficiency of modest rewards.

The quality of the Red Army in operations reflects these influences and attitudes. Fighter pilots, for example, are competent aviators but expect to be subject to close direction from ground control to an extent that their counterparts in the NATO air forces would resent. Compare the level of efficiency of an East German division undertaking a night bridging exercise in parallel with one of the group of Soviet forces in their country. The former retain a tradition of expecting leaders at all levels to carry forward orders but to adapt these as circumstances demand in order to achieve the aim. On numerous occasions a Russian division that should have built its bridges in darkness and be passing traffic across before dawn is still bridge building after first light while East German allies up or downstream, exercising under exactly the same conditions, have long completed their tasks. Though such manifestations do not suggest that the Red Army is not fit to go to war, it is evident that its ranks are not composed of supermen. It may account for the fact that they are most apprehensive of encountering the Federal German Army, that they respect next in order the Americans because of their technology, but doubt the staying power of the British because they lack depth of trained reserves. Overall, however, the available evidence suggests that the General Staff in Moscow does not regard the fighting forces of NATO, conventional and nuclear, a pushover.

Exercise scenarios for the Warsaw Pact forces invariably open with an attempt by NATO forces to attack across their frontiers from which they are at once pushed back by a counter-offensive. So goes the opening narrative. As earlier remarked, the Red Army and Eastern Bloc forces are organised and trained for aggression. But how will the high command convince the forces first that a NATO onslaught is imminent, when it will not be, and second that it has taken place when nothing has occurred? Almost any tarrydiddle sufficed as an excuse for crossing the frontiers into Poland in 1939 – the explanation to the junior ranks that they were 'going to the aid of Polish workers' was never called into question and was scarcely heeded by forces with a low standard of education, accustomed as they were to simple obedience in those days and close to campaigns of terror and the philosophy that the leadership knows best. The advances in the education of Russian youth, and their knowledge of the Western world, may still be fragmentary or seen through a glass darkly, but they will not so easily be fooled. Highly patriotic young men who would fight heroically for their motherland may not be so keen to suffer, much less to risk death, if they have an uneasy suspicion that they are pawns in a monstrous hoax.

And what of the conscript members of the Polish, Czechoslova- kian or Hungarian forces? For that matter, what of the youth recruited from Lithuania, Latvia and Estonia, whether serving a first term with the colours at the outbreak of war or recalled from the reserve on mobilisation? Their level of education is rising; their access to information about the other half of Europe and of North America grows. Many of them have been brought up by parents who have known what it is like to live in a democratic society. They will not be easily gulled by manifestly false stories from the propaganda machine that NATO invaders – West Germans, Americans and, least likely of all, Dutch or Belgians – are on their soil. How will young East Germans be convinced that their western frontier has been broken open by the British when the massive barbed-wire fences and other obstacles separating them are still intact? Although the role of the satellite forces in a Warsaw Pact offensive would be complementary, it would not be unimportant and it would involve many of them in combat. There must be doubts about the degree of their ardour in fighting battles for the benefit of Russia.

Armaments burdens, manpower difficulties, problems of train- ing and motivation militate progressively for the Soviet Union towards a conclusion that peace and disarmament are strongly in its interest. But however evident this may be to observers in the Atlantic Alliance, it is not a simple choice for those holding power in the Kremlin. Reduction to a purely defensive capability might be objectionable to some of the *nomenklatura* because it would involve acceptance, inescapably manifest, that Russia was not menaced by the Western democracies. It would also involve acceptance that war or the threat of it could no longer be used at an opportune moment to conduct foreign policy. It might be concluded that the only means remaining to further the international socialist struggle would be propaganda and subversion.

It is not likely that these everyday tools would be readily abandoned. They have been an inseparable part of international Communism under the leadership of the Soviet Union, the legacy of the founding fathers, notably Lenin among the Russians; the prime means of carrying forward the armed struggle by which the workers seize power. It remains a canon of Marxism/Leninism that governments in capitalist states, though they may be bourgeois democracies, will not yield power peacefully. Revolution arising from the 'class struggle' is still the only respectable method of securing change; evolution is a heresy currently advocated by misguided if not downright treacherous Eurocommunists.

Yet, for the growing number of new men in the Kremlin, the use of propaganda, overt and covert, and subversion will surely not be considered adequate as a means of bringing the world progressively into the socialist camp. For one thing, they have failed to do so to date. Subventions to potential revolutionary organisations or agencies have rarely paid a dividend of any significance. A more fruitful course, without excluding the continuance to these purely political activities, would be to return to Khrushchev's idea of surpassing the capitalist world in the material wealth of citizen and state.

A strategy of this nature could only succeed, however, if the constraints which denied success to Khrushchev were removed. Gorbachev perceives that the relationship between state, management and workers must change if there is to be a correction in, for example, manufacturing industry, of the system which makes faulty goods cheaply or high-class items at uneconomic prices. This would involve not only greater encouragement of individual responsibility but also the practice of it. It would involve adaptation to the usages of the free market-place.

Where such changes would lead is uncertain. The devolution of responsibility necessitates a devolution of power and the extension of liberty of action. The Soviet Union is rooted in centralism. It may prove to be adaptable in some degree to the new ideas but the structure of party government, and society will clearly be subjected to great strains if they are implemented.

There is none the less a linkage between reduction in armaments and military manpower, and the unbinding of the economy. The first would free resources for trade and industry. Those resources will not be exploited effectively unless *glasnost* and *peristroika* are carried through wholeheartedly.

Russian self-interest suggests that, dangers notwithstanding, some measure of disarmament is becoming attractive to Gorbachev and the men who support him closely, a twin pillar of policy with that of internal reform. Each movement towards realisation of these policies affords the Atlantic powers a glimpse of peace.

# CHAPTER TWENTY

# PEACE IS A CONDITION OF INFINITE FRAGILITY

Return to the Kremlin. Pass below the onion towers, through the great walls until, finally, through splendid double doors, the *Politburo* – judging by the numbers, perhaps just its most powerful executive – is found in session again, discussing foreign policy. For all its perils, the journey is worth making because it is important to discover from this centre of authority whether the leadership is committed to a peaceful solution of the conflict between Communism and capitalism.

In the West some say, 'Of course they want peace. If they conquered us, how would they hold the whole of western Europe down?' Hitler knew the answer to that. He did it for a long time with quite small forces. There were adequate numbers aspiring to the appointment of national *Gauleiter*, to work directly in the interests of the Third *Reich*, just as today there are numbers of national commissars in waiting, and by no means only the current members of the far-Left spectrum of political life. With modern satellite, infra red and acoustic technology to complement the tactics of terror, it would not be difficult to bring the European democracies to the status of Czechoslovakia or Poland, whose peoples once enjoyed political liberty, for more years than those conquered would care to think about.

Equally, it is pointless to assert that the Russians want to proceed peacefully precisely because the North American states and their European allies are peaceable. North America and the states of Europe and Asia were attacked by Germany and Japan whether they wanted war or not. Besides, it is not a matter of the Russians as individuals wanting to start hostilities. Ask any private citizen next time you are in Moscow or, say, Chernobyl, if they want war. Without the least insincerity they will say they do not. The private citizen is not the problem. The problem is with the Communist Party of the Soviet Union and the government apparatus which it instructs; the party which controls so closely the lives of all those private citizens.

So the question should be looked at seriously: is the leadership committed to a peaceful solution of the conflict between Communism and capitalism or, as the members of the Atlantic Alliance would put it, between Communism and democracy?

Here is Dmitri Manuilski speaking to party cadres in the Lenin School of Political Warfare in Moscow in 1931.

War to the hilt between Communism and capitalism is inevitable. Today, of course, we are not strong enough to attack. Our time will come in twenty or thirty years. To win we need the element of surprise. The bourgeoisie will have to be put to sleep. So we shall begin by launching the most spectacular peace movement on record. There will be electrifying overtures and unheard-of concessions. The capitalist countries, stupid and decadent, will rejoice to co-operate in their own destruction. They will leap at another chance to be friends. As soon as their guard is down, we shall smash them with our clenched fist.

Although more than half a century has passed since it was expressed, the same idea has been repeated in various forms almost up to the present time. Some zealots among officials and military officers still regard the strategy highly because they are fundamentalists in the teachings of Marx and Lenin. These are the men and women who have kept active the direction that the indoctrination of Soviet citizens must inculcate 'a spirit of hatred towards the imperialists...the enemies of Communism', a quotation from *Sovetskiy patriot* in May 1971, but by no means the last of such assertions, even if the language has been less explicit in more recent times. In 1987, *Ogonyek*, a popular magazine, published letters reminding readers that in Stalin's time the nation was better ordered, crime, especially 'hooliganism', was negligible and work discipline of a high order. Fundamentalism is far from dead.

Then there are those who believe that they are actively menaced by the capitalists, including those who are bourgeois democrats. It seems highly probable that some members of the *Politburo* fear an attack by NATO, though their best military intelligence indicates that the governments concerned lack the power to initiate an aggressive war and the NATO forces lack the physical means of launching a conventional offensive with any hope of success. They know yet more certainly that any attempt at a surprise nuclear attack would be suicidal for the initiator. For them, fear triumphs over knowledge and reason. They are the victims of their environment, their own propaganda.

Yet there are others, members of the old tradition who have lived or travelled extensively abroad, who have come to other conclusions. Viktor Nekrasov, an architect turned novelist, who took part in the epic battle for Stalingrad during the Second World War, wrote in the *Sunday Telegraph* in 1974,

> ...I fought for my country and for my people and for an unknown lad called Vitya. I hoped that Vitya would become a musician, a poet, or simply a man. But I did not fight so that, when he grew up, that boy should come to me with a warrant, dig through my archives, search my visitors and try to teach me his idea of patriotism.

Khrushchev believed that Nekrasov's writing about the world beyond the Iron Curtain did 'not recognise the demands of the party', and called for his expulsion from the writers' union. But perhaps a greater problem for the fundamentalists is that it is not only older people who have come to see that the demands of the party are corrupting, but also a younger element. These people, beneficiaries of the expansion of higher education, have been able to reflect upon a broader experience and outlook; to ponder which predictions have proved right, why capitalism has been in 'its final crisis' so long, what has and has not been successful in past policies; to consider the shortcomings of daily life and to ask themselves what prevents them being remedied. Reaching certain conclusions, these men and women, along with others of older generations, find themselves riding a tiger. It is plain to them that getting off will be difficult.

Some optimistic politicians and political commentators in the Atlantic Alliance seem to believe that Gorbachev has embarked upon a chain of internal reforms that will lead inexorably and in the short term to a form of social democracy. Some evidently think that he may be pushed by the criticism of the outside world into such a course. These views are not informed by the history of Russia and the character of its development since 1917, notwithstanding the manifestations of those Soviet men and women who wish to break out of the mould of narrow orthodoxy. Suppose that the fairy godmother, Atlanta, delivered a political magic wand to the NATO heads of state in conference in Brussels and that it was at once waved towards eastern Europe. Suppose the result was the release of reason and the *Politburo* was duly irradiated by the benevolent light; that they at once became convinced that Marxism-Leninism was not an infallible prescription for proceeding by stages to Utopia. The result would not then be an onrush of Soviet delegates with chain-cutters to the Eastern Bloc countries, or a mission to Brussels charged to say: 'You are right, we are wrong. Democracy rules, OK.' There would be no sign, internally, of the early abandonment of single-party rule. The unshackling of minds and attitudes in a great state which has never known true democratic process, and orderly progress to adoption of that method of government, would take a very long time. In any case, change in the political structure of the Soviet Union is a matter for its citizens, however difficult it may be for them to bring it about.

Still, no magic wand has arrived in Brussels. It has not been re-directed to Washington. There is, though, this consolation: the United States, spokesman for itself but also for its allies, is engaged in the most promising negotiations since the Second World War, if not precisely to disarm, then to lower the level of armaments and military manpower. It has entered these with reservations because of the Soviet Union's past record for evasion and duplicity, embracing attempts to use negotiations as a means of securing military advantage. But it is now evident that Russian material self-interest is involved in a reduction of war potential as much as that of the Atlantic Alliance, given mutual and balanced reductions in nuclear capability and conventional strength.

Mutual and balanced reductions, these are the principles to be observed if the present armed stability is not to be upset. 'Balance' is a reminder that NATO needs to preserve sufficient nuclear forces, tactical as well as strategic, to compensate for its inferiority in conventional strength until the conventional advantage of the Warsaw Pact has been brought into equilibrium. Otherwise, options might be opened to the Soviet Union whereby a military advantage could be exploited by a sudden and irrecoverable weakness inflicted on itself by NATO. Such a view does not necessarily impugn Mr Gorbachev's good faith. Failure to ensure mutuality and balance as the levels of armed power declined might persuade an opposition group among his associates – including those from the KGB and armed forces – made anxious by the whole range of changes accomplished or contemplated in party and government, that the violent overthrow of imperialism would dispose of external and internal enemies simultaneously. The risk would be that NATO might not succumb but that would simply result in a return to the discipline and frugality of more familiar times. A Russian sergeant, preparing to return home from Bulgaria at the end of the Second World War, was asked by a British liaison officer in Sofia how he and his family would survive in the scorched countryside. 'We can eat roots,' he said. 'We have done it before.'

Those of the *nomenklatura* who felt their position was threatened, or who were racked by emotion at the apparent abandonment of the philosophy which they regarded as inviolable and sacrosanct, might judge that their people were not so far divorced from their past by hamburgers, pop music and jeans that they could not, if necessary, be induced to eat roots for a while. They might be right.

The danger of the Atlantic Alliance being hustled or drawn into premature measures of disarmament will be heightened by each successive stage of agreement between the two sides. The history of United States international negotiations since the war has been characterised by the impetuosity of its political leaders and their supporters, the product of a yearning for action and accomplishment heightened so often by the approach of one sort of election or another. Many secretaries of state have shown the ability to play their hands shrewdly but all too often have had their authority usurped. Hustle and bustle are not conducive to making sound contracts, whether buying a house or peace.

The pacifist lobby will press the moral splendour of unilateralism on presidents and prime ministers. Somewhat more persuasively, the arguments of departmental secretaries and ministers, closely briefed by their financial advisers, will remark on the advantages of early savings in defence budgets. Memoranda will multiply indicating that cutting a corner here and taking a long view there would save substantial sums of money without incurring, from the point of view of the pocket calculators, undue risk. Party advantage will not weigh only among those in government; an option for defence savings is a useful stick to lay about the shoulders of cabinet members.

Those who have the responsibility of governmental office in NATO should keep this consideration in mind. The military strength of the organisation at the outset of negotiations is barely adequate for deterrence on the basis of a nuclear and conventional mix of forces. Impetuous gestures to satisfy or trump populists at home will not serve their nation and may ruin it if balance is not preserved. Dramatic options such as beaching all submarines and aircraft carriers, scrapping all tanks, strike aircraft and any instrument that seems to possess an offensive capability may well be proposed by well-meaning advocates but should be courteously declined. Options such as reductions in military service or the slicing of weapons and equipment programmes which are already threadbare will be just as dangerous to national security in the last quarter of the twentieth century as they were in the second. Reductions of this kind whet the appetite of Russians with a taste for military opportunism as much as once they did for Germans with a similar partiality.

Strength of resolve and vigilance are also needed in the complementary field of verification that disarmament measures agreed on are being adhered to. During earlier negotiations, the NATO view, with some dissentients, has tended to be a simple one: we are ready to admit Soviet inspectors into our territory on challenge providing that they will give us the same right of access. Advances towards agreement on the abandonment of intermediate nuclear weapons have obliged the Atlantic Alliance negotiators to examine precise arrangements for verification more closely.

Satellite photography will detect the deployment of any new missile after dismantling has been accomplished, and with radio monitors would pick up flying tests of any new models which might be developed secretly. But during the process of dismantling and in the period thereafter, there will be a need for checking on the ground by military inspectors. This will almost certainly necessitate admission to sites which are sensitive because they included high technology of another kind. Such difficulties throughout the whole range of progressive disarmament will require painstaking and probably slow evolution of safeguards and subsequent negotiation of their acceptance by each side.

A successful outcome is possible, probable even, given the mutuality of interest by those working for it. There may well come a time, then, when the NATO and Warsaw Pact nuclear and conventional forces have been substantially reduced and are in balance. That is the objective: total disarmament is not envisaged because it is not feasible given the present political polarity. Dangers will persist.

The economies of scale and range of weaponry will have benefited taxpayers throughout the Atlantic Alliance but the consequent enjoyment will be short-lived. Soon there will come demands for further 'savings' – the professional phrase – in the defence budget. In any nation in which such demands are compelling, the armed forces will then marched down a well-trodden road. The defence secretary, aware that there is no capacity for reduction in the budget protests to the Treasury. His protest is overridden. He warns that the scale of economy required will necessitate the removal of major items from the equipment programme – a number of aircraft or several frigates, reductions that cannot be hidden. The Cabinet view is that this would be intolerably damaging to its standing; 'savings' must be made in such a way as to preserve the appearance of adequately manned, well-equipped and well-administered defence forces. With that caveat, the remit is passed to the chiefs of staff. It is put about that the decision as to precisely how savings are to be effected will be made by the professional heads of the services. But in such circumstances, these luckless men have only one option: the process of 'salami-slicing'. The Treasury will help them by declaring a figure for inflation in the next financial year which falls significantly short of actuality. The next annual budget will therefore be starting from a reduced base. Slicing has started. It may not take off a limb or nose; they would be readily missed. A finger or two, some toes or part of an ear would not be observed or might be explained as a temporary oddity. It will be necessary to take something from every programme: flying hours are up for shaving once more, so too are scales of training ammunition, exercises, renewal of operational ammunition stocks grown antique and often dangerous to store. Recruiting limitations will be imposed for regular forces; where there is compulsory service, the term will be shortened. Allowances will not increase to take account of inflation. The replacement of outdated equipment will be postponed. Such measures as these put the Norwegian forces into action against Hitler's *Wehrmacht* in 1940 with artillery manufactured in the nineteenth century, sent British armoured forces to France at the outset of war with numerous vehicles sheathed in plywood instead of steel, denied the forces in Malaya fighters to match the Japanese air attack or the defenders of the Philippines an effective anti-aircraft defence. They were responsible for the fielding of poorly trained servicemen against highly trained troops. However good the safeguards built into a mutual and balanced reduction in armaments between the NATO and Warsaw Pact members may be, they will be valueless if elements of the former thereafter gratuitously weaken their capacity for deterrence.

But the desire for defence 'savings' will not be the only means whereby the Atlantic Alliance may demonstrate an inability to resist armed aggression. The immediate reduction in apparent threat will surely revive proposals that NATO at least, if not the Alliance as a grouping of like-minded states, should be disbanded and the United States remove its forces from Europe. Several political parties in western European states, on the far Left and a few on the far Right, which might well become members of a coalition government in their native countries, declare this to be a part of their policy. The United States government might feel obliged to heed internal demands for withdrawal from the tiresome and ungrateful old continent. Those who ask how friendly nations, neighbours in the democratic tradition, should by association protect their interests will be pointed towards the United Nations organisation. But if the UN has proved more enduring than the League of Nations, its capacity for restraining aggression has declined as its membership has grown. This is the body which has failed to contain Libya during its interference in the affairs of North African states and the excesses of Libyan and associated terrorists in Europe. Members of the United Nations have been unable to agree on measures to halt the breaches of international law perpetrated by the Ayatollah's regime in Iran or the fragmentation of the Lebanon by outsiders. It is the United States – not the United Nations – which has pressed the Soviet Union to leave Afghanistan to its own affairs.

Thus, however successful the negotiations for a reduction of nuclear and conventional forces in Europe, the Atlantic Alliance and the North Atlantic Treaty Organisation should be kept in operation so long as the Communist Party of the Soviet Union or any other single party in the state maintains its hegemony and, internally, does not offer its people regularly the opportunity to turn it out of office and put in new men and women of their choice from some quite different political persuasion; so long as the party in power has the means to commit its peoples to an aggressive war.

Those who live in liberty, especially those who have enjoyed liberty for generations and take it for granted, tend to believe that their condition is the norm, that others governed by despots are only temporarily disadvantaged. They are mistaken. The greater number of peoples in the world are deprived of political liberty. Similarly, those who believe that civilised peoples can no longer be brought to fight one another are in error. This was the view of the victors at the end of the First World War. Just over twenty years later, the greater part of the world was entering a new war involving even greater destruction, misery, and deprivation. Of course, present circumstances are not exactly the same as those leading up to the 'falling into war' in 1914 or the contrived opening rounds of 1939–41. History does not repeat itself in precise patterns. But nations no less than persons are prone to continue to make the mistakes which stem from their character and to suffer the same penalties if they do not take care.

A third world war in this century has been avoided to date by the initiative of a few great men in 1948 who saw to it that the democracies did not return to their old and foolish habits of combining a false idealism with *laisser faire*. In the process of abandoning the deterrence of arms, the product of their wisdom, extraordinary care must be taken to ensure that, as a consequence, a memorably long period of European security does not come to an end. Peace is an infinitely fragile condition.

# SELECT BIBLIOGRAPHY

The following represents a selection of the published works on which I have drawn.

**Europe, 1919–40**

Abshagen, K.H., *Canaris*, Stuttgart, 1949.
Ambrosius, H.H., *Unser Kampf in Norwegen*, Hamburg, 1940.
Baines, Norman H., ed.,*The speeches of Adolf Hitler, April, 1922–August, 1939*, two vols, New York, 1942.
Bathe, R., *Der Kampf um die Nordsee: Chronik des Luft-und-Seekrieges im Winter 1939–40 und des Norwegischen Feldzuges*, Oldenburg, 1940.
Benes, Eduard, *Memoirs of Dr Eduard Benes*, London, 1954.
Benoist-Mechin, J., *History of the German Army Since the Armistice, vol I, From the Imperial Army to the Reichswehr*, Paris, 1939.
Bethell, N., *The War Hitler Won, September, 1939*, London, 1972.
Bohlen, Charles, E., *Witness to History 1929–1969*, New York and London, 1973.
Buchner, A., *Narvik: Die Kämpfe der Gruppe Dietl im Frühjahr, 1940*, Heidelberg, 1958.
Bullitt, William C., *For the President, Personal and Secret: Correspondence Between Franklin D. Roosevelt and William C. Bullitt*, Boston, 1972.
Bullock, Alan, *Hitler: A Study in Tyranny*, London, 1952.
Busch, F.O., *Kampf im Norwegens Fjorde: Fall Weserübung Nord*, Holstein, 1964.
Cadogan, Sir A., *The Diaries of Sir Alexander Cadogan, 1938–45*, New York and London, 1972.
Carr, Edward Hallett, *German–Soviet Relations Between the Two World Wars, 1919-39*, London, 1952.
Carsten, F.L., *The Reichswehr and Politics, 1918–33*, Oxford, 1966.
Churchill, Sir Winston, *The Second World War*, vol I, Boston and London, 1948.
Cole, Wayne S., *Roosevelt and the Isolationists, 1932–45*, Lincoln, University of Nebraska Press, 1983.
Cork and Orrery, Admiral of the Fleet the Earl of, 'Norway Campaign, 1940', *London Gazette Supplement*, 1947.
Dahlerus, Birger, *The Last Attempt*, London, 1947.
Derry, Dr. T.K., *The Campaign in Norway, 1940*, London, 1952.
'Documents on British Foreign Policy, 1919–39,' United Kingdom official series, (London), 1947–71.
'Documents on German Foreign Policy, 1919–45,' United States official series, (Washington), 1957.
'Documents and Materials Relating to the Eve of the Second World War, 1937–39,' Soviet Union official publication, (Moscow), 1948.
'Documents Concerning German–Polish Relations and the Outbreak of Hostilities Between Great Britain and Germany', United Kingdom official publication, (London),1939.
Feiling, Keith, *The Life of Neville Chamberlain*, London, 1946.
Feingold, Henry L., *The Politics of Rescue: The Roosevelt Administration and the Holocaust, 1938–45*, New Brunswick, New Jersey, 1970.
Frischauer, Willy, *Goering*, London, 1951.

Galland, Adolf, *The First and the Last: The Rise and Fall of the Luftwaffe Fighter Forces, 1938–45*, London, 1955.

Gilbert, Martin S., *Biography of Winston S. Churchill: vol V, 1922–39, and companion vol, 'The Wilderness Years', vol VI, Finest Hour*, London, 1981 and 1983.

Goerlitz, Walter, *History of the German General Staff, 1657–1945*, New York, 1953.

Gordon, H.J., *The Reichswehr and the German Republic, 1919–1926*, New York, 1957.

Grew, Joseph, *Turbulent Era: a Diplomatic Record of Fifty Years, 1904–45*, Boston, 1952.

Guderian, Heinz, *Panzer Leader*, London, 1952.

Halder, Franz, *Hitler als Feldherr*, Munich, 1949.

Halifax, Earl of, *Fullness of Days*, London, 1957.

Hauge, Andreas, *Kampene i Norge, 1940*, Oslo, 1978.

Hibbert, Christopher, *Mussolini*, London, 1962.

Hull, Cordell, *The Memoirs of Cordell Hull*, New York, 1948.

Macintyre, D.F.G.W., *Narvik*, London, 1959.

Manstein, Erich von, *Lost Victories*, London, 1958.

Mellenthin, F.W. von, *Panzer Battles, 1939–45*, London, 1955.

Morgan, J.H., *Assize of Arms: Germany and Her Re-armament, 1919–39*, London, 1945.

Morgan, Ted, *FDR; A Biography*, New York and London, 1986.

Namier, Sir L., *Diplomatic Prelude*, London, 1948.

Neugebauer, N.M., *The Defence of Poland, September, 1939*, London, 1942.

O'Neill, R.J.P., *The German Army and the Nazi Party, 1933–39*, London, 1966.

Pogue, Forrest, C., *George C. Marshall: Ordeal and Hope*, New York, 1966.

Reed, Douglas, *The Burning of the Reichstag*, New York, 1934.

Schuschnigg, Kurt von, *Austrian Requiem*, Zurich, 1946, London, 1947.

Shirer, William L., *The Rise and Fall of the Third Reich*, London, 1960.

Taylor, A.J.P., *The Course of German History*, London, 1945.

Taylor, T., *Sword and Swastika: the Wehrmacht in the Third Reich*, London, 1953.

Tugwell, Rexford G., *The Democratic Roosevelt: A Biography of Franklin D. Roosevelt*, Philadelphia, New York, 1957.

Wheeler-Bennett, Sir J. *The Nemesis of Power*, London, 1953.

Zaloga, S.J., *The Polish Campaign, 1939*, London, 1985.

**The Onset and Event of War in the Far East**

Beasley, W.G., *Modern History of Japan*, London, 1963.

Bennett, H. Gordon, *Why Singapore Fell*, Sydney, 1944.

Bernstein, David, *The Philippine Story*, New York, 1947.

Borg, Dorothy, *The United States and the Far Eastern Crisis of 1933–38*, Cambridge, Mass., 1964.

Brereton, Lewis H., *The Brereton Diaries*, New York, 1946.

Brook-Popham, Sir R., 'Operations in the Far East from 17th October, 1940, to 27th December, 1941', *London Gazette Supplement*, 1948.

Clement, E.W., *A Short History of Japan*, London, 1936.

Conroy, R., *The Battle of Bataan: America's Greatest Defeat*, Toronto, 1969.

Falk, S.L., *Seventy Days to Singapore: the Malayan Campaign, 1941–42*, London, 1975.

Friend, Theodore, *Between Two Empires*, New Haven, 1965.

Frye, William, *Marshall, Citizen Soldier*, Indianapolis, 1947.

Grenfell, R., *Main Fleet to Singapore*, London, 1951.

Hamill, I., *The Strategic Illusion: The Singapore Strategy and the Defence of Australia and New Zealand, 1919–42*, London, 1981.

Hamilton, Sir Ian, *A Staff Officer's Scrapbook*, London, 1912.

Hayashi, S., *Kogun: The Japanese Army in the Pacific War*, Quantico, Va., 1959.

Horner, F.J., *A Case History of Japan*, London, 1948.

Huff, Sidney, 'My Fifteen Years with General MacArthur', *Saturday Evening Post*, Sep–Oct, 1951.

James, D. Clayton, *The Years of MacArthur, vols I and II*, Boston, 1970 and 1975.

Kirby, S.W., *The War Against Japan, vol I, The Loss of Singapore*, London, 1957.

Lewin, Ronald, *The American Magic*, New York and London, 1982.

Liu, F.F., *A Military History of Modern China, 1924–49*, Princeton, 1956.

Long, Gavin, *MacArthur as Military Commander*, London, 1969.

Lory, H. *Japan's Military Masters*, New York, 1943.

Maltby, P.C., *Report on Air Operations in Malaya*, London Gazette Supplement, 1948.

Manchester, William, *American Caesar: Douglas MacArthur, 1880–1964*, New York and London, 1978–9.

Millis, Walter, *The War Reports of General of the Army George C. Marshall, General of the Army H.H. Arnold, and Fleet Admiral Ernest J. King*, Philadelphia, 1947.

Nakamura, K., *History of Japan*, Tokyo, 1939.

Neumann, William L., *America Encounters Japan: From Perry to MacArthur*, Baltimore, 1963.

Percival, A.E., *Operations in Malaya Command from 8th December, 1941, to 15th February, 1942*, London Gazette Supplement, 1948.

Reel, A. Frank, *The Case of General Yamashita*, Chicago, 1971.

Reischauer, E.O., *Japan: The Story of a Nation*, London, 1970.

Swinson, A., *Defeat in Malaya*, London, 1970.

Tsuji, M., *Singapore: The Japanese Version*, London, 1962.

United Service Institution of India, *The Campaign in Malaya, 1941–42*, New Delhi, 1960.

United States Department of the Army, *History of the Army in World War II, The War in the Pacific. The Fall of the Philippines*, Washington, 1953.

# INDEX